This is indeed India! The land of dreams
and romance, of fabulous wealth and
fabulous poverty, of splendour and rags, of
palaces and hovels, of famine and
pestilence, of genii and giants and Aladdin
lamps, of tigers and elephants, the cobra
and the jungle, the country of a hundred
nations and a hundred tongues, of a
thousand religions and two million gods,
cradle of the human race, birthplace of
human speech, mother of history,
grandmother of legend, great-grandmother
of traditions, whose yesterdays bear date
with the smouldering antiquities of the rest
of the nations – the one sole country
under the sun that is endowed with an
imperishable interest for alien prince
and alien peasant, for lettered and
ignorant, wise and fool, rich and poor,
bond and free, the one land that all
men desire to see, and having seen once, by
even a glimpse, would not give that
glimpse for the shows of all the rest of the
globe combined.

Mark Twain

india **modern**

Traditional Forms and Contemporary Design

Herbert J.M. Ypma

To Pryna Ypma

Pages 2-7:
Although not significant in any way architecturally, these
photographs, randomly taken from everyday life, reveal ubiquitous
qualities deeply embedded in Indian creative expression. Namely, the
importance of colour, the repetition of a simple geometric form, and
the presence of the square (a shape that since ancient times has been
used by the Hindus to symbolize man in relation to the universe).

Phaidon Press Limited
Regent's Wharf
All Saints Street
London N1 9PA

First published 1994
First paperback edition 1997
© 1994 Phaidon Press Limited

This edition first published 2000
© 2000 Phaidon Press Limited

ISBN 0 7148 3948 5

A CIP catalogue record for this book is available from the British
Library.

Printed in China

Introduction

My first visit to India was in 1981. I was sent by a design company to instigate the design and development of some fabrics for a new range of contemporary furnishings. My brief was simple: I was to go to Panipat, a village a few hours north of Delhi, which had a reputation for making the type of fabrics we were interested in, and work together with the village foremen to finalize a range of fabrics that could be ordered for production. This experience created an impression of India that will stay with me forever. India was a visually sophisticated country with tremendous human resources and potential; a nation whose vast population of village craftsmen gives real meaning to the term skilled labour.

Ten years later India was back on my agenda. As publisher and editor of a design magazine called *Interior Architecture*, in its seventh year of publication, I instigated a complete change of editorial policy. We were to get off the 'what's new in Milan, Paris and London' bandwagon and set out on a path of real discovery. My manifesto for the new-look *Interior Architecture* was to look for design and design inspiration where other magazines wouldn't think to look: Polynesia, Mexico, Argentina, Vietnam, Bali, Morocco, Sicily, Zanzibar and, of course, India.

India was the first choice for these new issues. Everybody we contacted was excited about the project because, apparently, it was the first time that a magazine had proposed looking at contemporary design and architecture in India.

With an abundance of proposed material and the added bonus of generous sponsorship from the Indian Government, I set about planning what would turn out to be the most hectic month of my life.

My confidence in India was justified. We received incredible help and support everywhere we went. All the leads, directions and suggestions we had received proved, by and large, to be what we were looking for. India's architects and designers are not just busy making 'interesting shapes'. They are concerned with defining solutions in architecture and design that can answer some of the country's most pressing needs: how to preserve and maintain the relevancy of their craftsmen, how to allow India to live in the modern world without destroying its own distinctive heritage. It was quickly apparent that design plays more than an aesthetic role in India's culture.

It almost goes without saying that this excursion to India went too well! The amount of material we came back with was really too much for one magazine and it seemed a natural progression to suggest a book. India is such a wealthy country in terms of its culture that even a book can only *begin* to expose the beauty, history and creativity that exists there. *India Modern* is by no means a comprehensive work on the design culture of India. It was created to provide a brief but evocative glimpse of a side of India that many have never contemplated.

I

A Rich Reservoir

To be modern is not a fashion, it is a
state. It is necessary to understand
history, and he who understands history
knows how to find continuity between
that which was, that which is, and that
which will be.

Le Corbusier,
on the definition of 'modern'

A Rich Reservoir

It is difficult to imagine a more eloquent and universal definition of 'modern' than the one penned by one of this century's leading and most famous proponents of modernism, the Swiss architect Le Corbusier. People who identify with Le Corbusier as an unabashed modernist may be surprised by this statement, and may not have expected a man who was so concerned with the future to have had much regard for the past. But Le Corbusier travelled extensively throughout his career, and from the experiences he gained he came to realize the role that history plays in the architectural expression of a culture. History, he recognized, was the palette of the architect – the wealth of materials, colours, textures, forms and other choices from which works of lasting beauty are created. In the words of Balkrishna V. Doshi, an Indian architect who assisted Le Corbusier in India from 1952-60 with the design of the public buildings for the new capital of the Punjab at Chandigarh, we find a manifestation of these beliefs: Le Corbusier 'looked at the skyline of Indian temples, he saw arches and domes, verandas and balconies. He saw many things for the first time and in general I have the impression that in India he felt the impact of another culture that has joy and grace and compassion.'

Le Corbusier had the vision to recognize that one need not be restricted by a stereotypical three-dimensional model in order to be modern. Nor did he approve of the concept followed in many Western quarters of modern as a style and he fought against these misconceptions for much of the latter part of his career. His own definition of what is modern focuses on using elements of a culture's history to create contemporary forms of expression that reinforce rather than destroy links with the past.

India's history is unique. Despite numerous invasions, conquests and colonizations it has managed to maintain a sense of continuity in its culture while absorbing aspects of other cultures and allowing them to be superimposed onto its own like layers of tracing paper. So resilient have been its social and religious institutions, which have remained in place relatively unchanged for more than 4,000 years, that all attempts to radically alter or destroy them have been thrown off or absorbed, with the result that village life in India remains much the same today as it was thousands of years ago. Even in the fast-paced modern cities such as Bombay or Delhi, what appears to be a complete change of attitude and lifestyle is really only a surface veneer. Underneath, the age-old verities, loyalties and obligations, largely stemming from religion, still rule people's lives. There is possibly no other country in the world where religion is so inextricably linked with aspects of everyday life, and the origins of this intense spirituality stem from the very roots of Indian culture: to the birthplace of Hinduism and its accompanying mythology.

Mythology and Mathematics

The origins of Hinduism date from around 2500 BC to a culture which flourished along the Indus river valley, in what is now Pakistan.

Around 1500 BC Aryan forces swept down from central Asia bringing with them their own religious beliefs assimilated into the existing culture. People worshipped at fire altars built of intricately arranged layers of bricks which represented the relationship between man and the universe.

Although no significant example has survived from before the fifth century BC, the design concept of the fire altars has been discovered in the *Vedas* (sacred Hindu scriptures). When one contemplates the complexity of these altars, it is not surprising to learn that India is credited with the invention of mathematics. Made up of three altars constructed, respectively, in the form of a square (representing celestial space), a circle (symbolizing the terrestrial world) and a semi-circle (denoting the air world), each was surrounded by five layers of bricks; 21 bricks around the circle, 78 around the semi-circle and 260 surrounding the square. In all there were 396 bricks corresponding to the 360 days of the year plus a calendar month of 36 days. To complete the structure, and to finalize the equation, there were also 10,800 space-filling bricks that represented the hours in the year. On first impression it may be difficult to associate all this numerically-based geometry with spirituality, and especially with the tenets of the universal soul teachings of

Hinduism, but it is important to know that the image of man is central to the concept of these altars, the shape of which was modelled on the body of Cosmic Man.

The body of man, according to the Vedic scriptures, although important and significant, must ultimately be dissolved into a formless state. Cosmic Man, in his deconstructed state, provided the basis for an abstract numerical model which was used as a plan for the manifest world and in particular as a model for architecture. All architecture, therefore, whether sacred or secular, was consequently modelled on the concept of Cosmic Man and, in completion of an extraordinary cycle, everything created by man was symbolic of the cosmos, and the cosmos, in turn, was symbolic to man.

The *Vasta Purusha Mandala* is the name given to the mathematical model that restates the founding principles of the early Vedic priests and their fire altars; the *mandala* being a perfect square subdivided into identical squares, starting from 1, 4, 9, 16, 25 and continuing upwards to 1,024. In simple terms, these geometric configurations were used to determine the layout of a house, temple or an entire city. Thus from its beginning, Hindu culture used mathematics to devise a system of infinite applications and adaptations, and the *mandala* effectively allowed all architecture, private or public, small or large, to be based on a multiple of perfect squares.

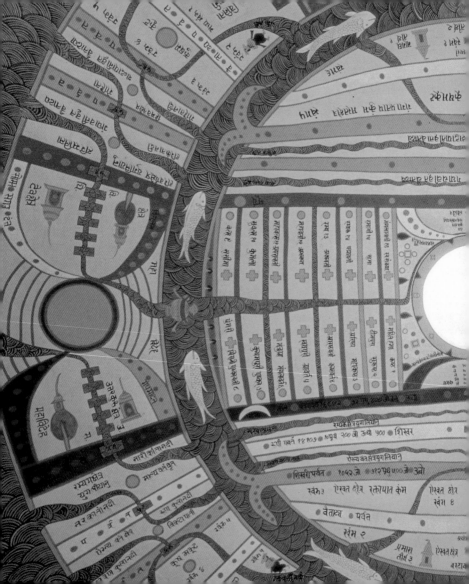

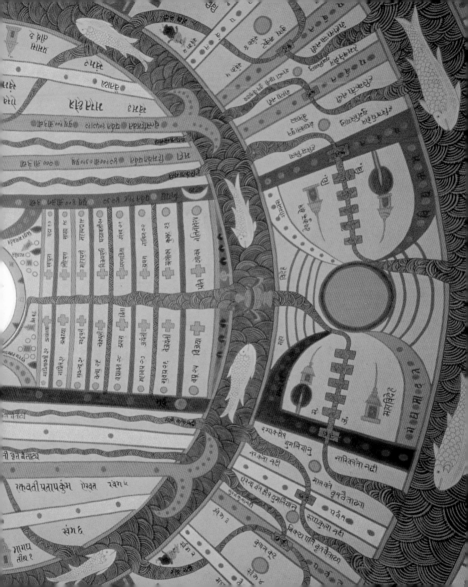

Subterranean Structures

There is perhaps no more unusual example of the relationship of Hindu myth to architecture than the unique phenomenon of India's subterranean structures known as stepwells. India's temples and palaces are well documented but these underground archaeological treasures seem to have been overlooked by most scholarly histories of India.

In Hindu mythology water is seen as the giver of life. Burrowing into the soil like a plough preparing a field for sowing, the stepwell transforms the path to water into a ritualistic pilgrimage and, through the establishment of an elaborate architectural structure, the daily chore of fetching water is turned into a spiritual experience.

Dating from the seventh century AD, the earliest stepwells – true to the concept of the *mandala* – were square in form. In essence inverted pyramids, the concentric square forms decreased in size as they descended into the earth's surface. As the form developed, the simple square forms gave way to more elaborate architectural expressions: bridges and landings were introduced as ingeniously conceived bracing elements between the parallel retaining walls of the structures, and what had once resembled a sunken village square now started to take on the complexity of structures above the ground.

Stepwells underwent a major metamorphosis with the arrival of the conquering Muslims in the twelfth century, when the forms became even more elaborate and imaginative. Islam brought its own mythological values to India and the ritualistic passage to water, also crucial to Muslim belief, was enhanced by the pleasure principle. Based on the Islamic concept of the Paradise Garden, or *Char Bagh*, the stepwells were transformed into pleasure pavilions. Delightfully cool rooms built within the underground passages, and looking down into a central void, provided a welcome respite from the heat. While retaining the rich symbolism attached to the water, these underground retreats, usually set within a garden, the focal point of which was an elaborate swimming pool, soon became the venue for musical soirées and poetry readings, as well as affairs of state.

Stepwells are elaborate architectural constructions built within the earth's surface. They make the path down to the water a ritualistic pilgrimage, a matter of profound metaphysical meaning considering water is seen as the giver of life.

Charles Correa

The Islamic Influence

Throughout history, India has shown an exceptional capacity to interact with outside influences, assimilating features from these new cultures into its own and allowing transformations to take place as if they had always meant to be there. Charles Correa, one of India's most acclaimed architects, defines transformation as change that involves 'absorption', 'internalization' and ultimately 'reinvention'. He is a firm believer in the role such transformations have played in India's development: 'When we look at the architectural heritage of India, we find an incredibly rich reservoir of mythic images and beliefs – each like a transparent overlay – starting with the models of the cosmos, right down to this century. And it is their continuing presence in our lives that creates the pluralistic society of India today.'

The most influential of these transformations occurred with the invasion of the Muslims in the twelfth century AD. Spreading eastwards from the crumbling Byzantine Empire, Islam conquered with ever increasing strength and momentum. But the Muslims were not slash and burn conquerors. Their passion for building heralded a golden age of architecture, arts and literature which resulted in some of the great masterpieces of Indian culture.

The Muslims brought their own myths with them to India, the most powerful of which was the concept of the *Char Bagh*, the Paradise Garden, an enduring feature of Persian art and architecture. Linked to a love of trees and flowers, the Paradise Garden represented a harmony between man and nature which was fundamentally symbolic of Muslim belief. In the *Char Bagh*, a plan of spiritual significance and mathematical symmetry, the main axis is a watercourse crossed at right angles by one or more secondary channels. The watercourses symbolize the four rivers of life and the intersections represent the meeting of man and God.

Spirituality and symmetry, the key ingredients of Hindu culture, proved also to be the basis of the invaders' culture, and so the conquering Muslims found not only a reinforcement of their own architectural order but also the possibility of adding another layer of meaning to their own established forms. Both sides gained from this encounter. Islamic culture brought with it elements that have enriched India's architectural vocabulary for centuries, such as the arch, the *jali* and the dome, and the ancient Hindu traditions of craft and a sophisticated grasp of mathematics, fuelled by powerful mythology, pushed Islamic architecture in India to previously unscaled heights.

The birth of Islam in the sands of
Saudi Arabia in the year 622 was
destined to divert, fundamentally,
the course of Indian history.
Never before in world history had
an idea proved so contagious and
politically potent.

Stanley Wolpert

Mughal Splendour

During the sixteenth century the Mughals, Muslims from central Asia, descended into India. Their invasion eventually led to a period of peaceful coexistence between Hindus and Muslims which favoured an unprecedented flowering of art and culture. The process of adoption and absorption, so familiar in India, was also nothing new to Islam. When the Muslims arrived in India they were confronted by a veritable embarrassment of riches: the finest marbles, the best metals, glorious gems and the most skilful and dedicated of craftsmen – treasures they gladly added to their own already impressive cultural repertoire. The Mughals utilized all of India's assets and added to them the many styles, techniques, technologies and traditions that they had adopted in the course of their conquests. Hence it was in India that the Muslims would realize a refinement and monumentality hitherto unheard of in the vast expanses of the Islamic empire.

It was the Emperor Shah Jahan (1592-1666), however, who built the most glorious monuments of Mughal rule, creating buildings of unimaginable splendour and beauty in the area around Delhi and Agra. Pure poetry in pristine white marble, the Taj Mahal at Agra was believed to have been constructed in memory of Shah Jahan's wife who died in childbirth, but recent translations of the inlaid calligraphy in the ceilings and walls reveal that the Taj Mahal was in fact an attempt to create the 'ultimate' building on earth: a model of the throne of God. Such was the power, confidence and glory enjoyed by the Mughal ruler at this time that he dared to get closer to God, almost tempting him to come down and enjoy what had been created in His honour. (In fact this brashness ultimately led to Shah Jahan's downfall: he was quickly deposed by his son who deplored his father's extravagance, especially in architecture.)

For the next 200 years Indian culture flourished: Muslim sultans and Hindu princes constructed extraordinary buildings and Hindu myths continued to develop. Still, however, the common motif of India's architectural heritage, the *mandala*, the guiding spiritual and mathematical model throughout India's history, remained at the heart of India's significant architectural monuments.

As the Englishman leaned out of the carriage he saw first an opal-tinted cloud on the horizon, and, later, certain towers. The mists lay on the ground, so that the splendour seemed to be floating free of the earth, and the mists rose in the background, so that at no time could everything be seen clearly. Then as the train sped forward, and the mists shifted, and the sun shone upon the mists, the Taj took a hundred new shapes, each perfect and each beyond description. It was the Ivory Gate through which all good dreams come: it was the realization of the gleaming halls of dawn that Tennyson sighs of: it was veritably the 'aspiration fixed', the 'sigh made stone' of a lesser poet; and over and above concrete comparisons, it seemed the embodiment of all things pure, all things holy, and all things unhappy. That was the mystery of the building.

Rudyard Kipling

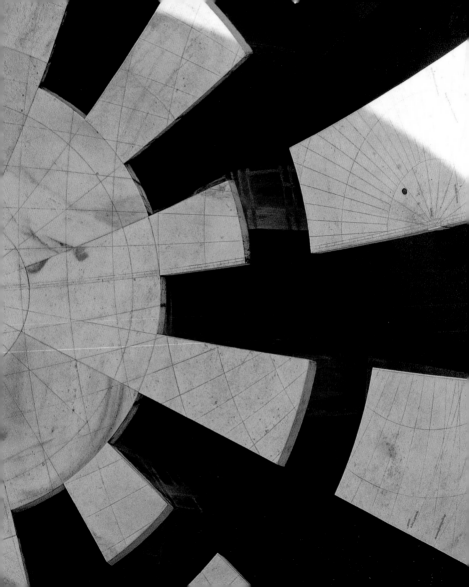

An Early Modernist

The city of Jaipur and the Jantar Mantar (the Jaipur Observatory), both designed by the great astronomer Maharaja Jai Singh II (1699–1744), represent another crucial and decisive transformation in India's cultural history.

These projects were the first attempt by an Indian ruler to combine ancient myths and sacred beliefs with the tenets of modern science. In his design for the city of Jaipur, Maharaja Jai Singh turned for inspiration to the basic nine-square *mandala* (corresponding to the *navagraha* or nine planets), a *pure* approach in historical terms and particularly as far as Hindu myths were concerned.

Unlike any previous *mandala*-based building, Maharaja Jai Singh applied the intuitive, logical intelligence of a scientist to adapt this plan to the topography of the area and to considerations generated by Islamic myths. To accommodate the presence of a hill, he used his grasp of mathematics and geometry to shift a square in the plan to the bottom and opposite end of the nine-square grid. In a similar way, the Islamic myth of the *Char Bagh* was accommodated by transforming the centre of the nine-square *mandala* into the garden of the city palace (instantly reinforcing the Hindu concept of Bindu, the centre of universe), and using the square immediately above it for the palace itself. As a result of Maharaja Jai Singh's interpretations of the ancient *mandala* form, the city is one of the most

functional examples of the implementation of this ancient diagram.

In his use of a simple geometrical plan, refined by a regard for function and efficiency, Maharaja Jai Singh can be considered as one of India's earliest 'modernists', and his purest expressions of modernism can be found in the buildings of the Jantar Mantar Observatory erected in, and at the same time as, the city of Jaipur. Used for making observations of celestial bodies, each astronomical instrument is a purpose-built structure used for following the path and marking the position of a particular star or group of stars. Observers would mount the steps of the carefully positioned structures after dark, and look for the reflection of a particular star or cluster of stars in the reflection basins constructed of polished white marble.

In seeking to synthesize the material and metaphysical worlds, and to build a relationship between the past and the future, Maharaja Jai Singh provided an important model for India's architecture. He proved that spiritualism, the basis of Indian culture, and science could not only coexist happily but when applied to architecture and design could also be a powerful creative force. However, it was not really until after India gained full independence that the Indian creative community began, in the words of Ram Rahman, to 'rediscover a sense of itself and learn from the lessons of its own history'.

Architecture is the pride of man, his triumph over gravitation, his will to power.

Friedrich Wilhelm Nietzsche

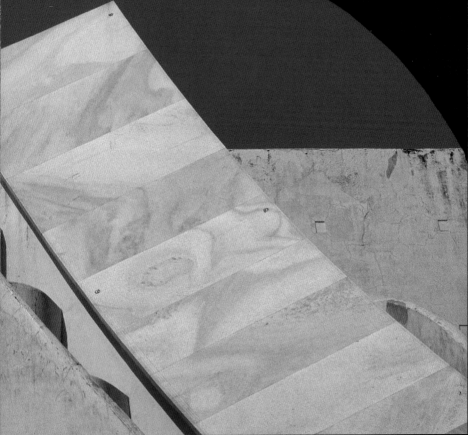

He [Maharaja Jai Singh II] was a pragmatic modernist who would have spared no effort to reach out for the best contemporary influence with which to realize his vision of the future.

Aman Nath

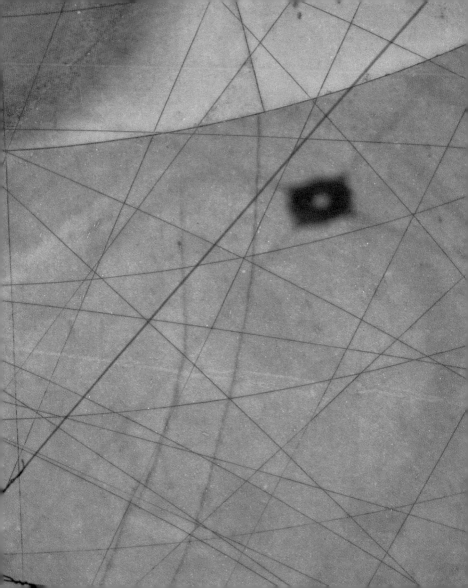

Colonialism

The arrival of the European colonial powers started a new and difficult period in the history of India. The values and aspirations of the Europeans were very different to those of the indigenous population. For example, the British, who first came as traders and by the early nineteenth century had become the largest colonial power on the subcontinent via the East India Company, were intent on exploiting and modernizing India for the benefit of the mother country. Railways began to be established in the 1850s and the most distant parts of India were soon linked together. Similarly ambitious projects were undertaken in building: the Victoria Terminus in Bombay, completed in 1878, was for a long time the largest covered railway station in the world. A work of great originality, it melded European Neo-Gothic forms with oriental and Saracenic motifs to form a style which became popularly known as 'Bombay Gothic'.

Despite numerous commendable public projects, however, little indigenous cultural development took place during the time of India's colonial rule. This is evident in the most ambitious of all architectural projects in the building of New Delhi. The architect selected to design the city, Sir Edwin Lutyens, never really came to terms with India's architectural heritage and it was only at the urging of the government that he sought to 'Indianize' his buildings. The result, a Buddhist-style dome on top of the Viceroy's palace, although impressive because of the sheer scale, is really nothing more than an architectural pastiche: a token application of a local idiom without any real understanding of its origin or meaning.

It was not really until the 1920s that the seeds for modern India were sown. The change was largely due to the influence of three men: Mahatma Gandhi, Rabindranath Tagore and Jawaharlal Nehru. Gandhi, the leader of the freedom struggle, had a firm understanding of the socio-economic realities of India's vast population (900 million), and as such he preached a return to the value-structure of the villages: simplicity, craftsmanship and independence from foreign power, both military and economic. Rabindranath Tagore, was the artist: a writer, painter and philosopher who initiated a cultural renaissance with the founding of an arts complex at Shantiniketan which re-established the classic *guru-shishya* relationship (emphasizing humanity's relationship with nature) and re-awakened traditional Indian attitudes to learning and knowledge. The youngest of the three, Jawaharlal Nehru, would become the first Prime Minister of independent India. He believed that India must industrialize and modernize or perish. It was Nehru who encouraged the selection of Le Corbusier as architect for the new city of Chandigarh, and it was he who understood that Le Corbusier's powerful vision of the future would act as a catalyst for the eventual emergence of contemporary Indian architecture.

PAGE 16
This view through a window to one of the courtyard gardens of Samode Palace, Rajasthan, serves as an appropriate visual metaphor for India's extraordinary history. Like the window into the garden, there is always the notion of 'looking beyond' as each subsequent vista of India's 4,000 year history reveals yet another complex layer of meaning.

PAGE 18
Patterned white clay on a mud house from one of the villages of Banni, Kutch, represents a decorative heritage that has changed little since Harrapian times (2500 BC). It is villages such as these, where the arrangement of the spaces corresponds to social structures (revealing the rituals and myths, cleverly seeded by the Brahmin of ancient times), which have kept Indian culture intact over the ages.

PAGES 20-21
A Jain cosmograph was the inspiration for a ceiling mural inside a domed pavilion at the Jawahar Kala Kendra Museum, Jaipur. The cosmograph is a metaphysical landscape, setting forth the ordering principles that are central to Jainism. One of three religions to have originated in India (along with Hinduism and Buddhism), Jainism is credited with the introduction into Hindu society of *ahimsa*, or nonviolence, a concept that Mahatma Gandhi would use almost 2,000 years later as an effective political tool.

PAGES 22-23
Jain nuns in the Tejpal Temple at Mount Abu, Rajasthan. Because of royal patronage, the temple emerged relatively early as India's classic architectural form. Like the ancient temples of Greece, temples in India were (and are) considered the 'home' of the deity which devotees visit with gifts and offerings (a practice known as *puja*). The Tejpal Temple c. 1230, is one of the Dilwara group of Jain temples renowned for exquisite marble carving.

PAGE 24
The earliest stepwells date from the seventh century. Strictly square in form, they are essentially inverted pyramids which descend into the earth. This stepwell is in the Rajasthani countryside.

PAGES 26-27
This stepwell at Osian, Rajasthan, was recently excavated to a depth of eight storeys. Stepwells are unique to India and reflect the spiritual significance of water in Hindu civilization. Their elaborate nature transformed the journey to water into a ritualistic pilgrimage.

PAGE 28
The Rajasamund Tank in Rajasthan, constructed in 1660. The height of the landings corresponds to the average height of a person so that after filling the pot with water, it is placed on a landing from where it is easily transferred to the head.

PAGE 30 Built to commemorate the arrival of Islam in India, the Qutb Minar in Delhi is an imposing structure built of ribbed and red sandstone. Overlaid with calligraphic inscriptions and encircled by ornate balconies, it was said, in the fourteenth century by Moorish traveller Ibn Battuta, to have 'no equal in all of Islam'.

PAGES 32-33 The 2,000-year-old Iron Pillar in Delhi, viewed through the Islamic arch that is part of the Quwwat-ul-Islam Mosque. The technology to stop the normally very quick oxidization of iron was not known at the time of its construction and thus how it was built and why it has never rusted remain a mystery.

PAGE 34
A worshipper amongst the pillars of the Quwwat-ul-Islam Mosque in Delhi. Constructed largely from pillars pillaged from Hindu temples, the mosque stands as a testament to the brutal assimilation of Hindu culture by the conquering Muslims.

PAGE 36
A detailed view of a marble courtyard in Akbar's tomb in Sikandra, a mausoleum built in memory of the Mughal emperor. This colonnade, with its golden play of light through the carved marble *jali*, introduces two innovations that were to become the hallmark of Mughal architecture: the extensive use of marble, and the inlay work of precious and semi-precious stones.

PAGE 38
Built by Emperor Shah Jahan (1592-1666) in the seventeenth century, there is no mistaking the dazzling white brilliance of the Taj Mahal. Arguably the finest example of Islamic architecture in the world, it reflects the heights reached when the Muslims assimilated the finest and strongest aspects of Hindu and Persian culture to create the splendour that we know as Mughal architecture.

PAGES 40-41
A view through the *jali* marble colonnade to one of the gates of Akbar's tomb, Sikandra. Set in a large garden, it is guarded by four red sandstone gates representing different faiths: one Hindu, one Muslim, one Christian and one of a religion of Akbar's own invention.

PAGE 42
Jai Prakash Yantra, the massive masonry hemisphere sunk into the ground at the Jantar Mantar observatory, Jaipur. Used for marking the position of the stars, it represents an attempt to combine ancient belief with the tenets of modern science.

PAGE 45
One of the stone instruments, part of a collection of 12 known as the Rashivalaya Yantra, that were used at the Jantar Mantar. Each instrument corresponds to a sign of the zodiac and is, in essence, a purpose-built observation tower.

PAGES 46-47
Indian interest in astronomy dates back to Vedic times (1500 BC). Three thousand years later, Jai Singh's dissatisfaction with the accuracy of available instruments led him to construct his own giant observation and measuring machines in stone and mortar.

PAGE 48
The sculptural slabs that constitute Jai Singh's astronomical instruments at the Jantar Mantar are early examples of pure 'modernist' architecture, where form is a direct translation of function. An observer would climb to the top of the steps and track the celestial bodies' reflections in the curved ruler of white marble slabs.

PAGES 50-51
The reflecting basin of the hemispherical Jai Prakash Yantra reveals the mathematical precision of the inscribed path markers and the utilization of suspended wires equipped with focal masks to increase accuracy.

PAGE 52
Victoria Terminus, Bombay, designed by F.W. Stephens. At the time of its construction, in 1878, it was the largest covered railway station in the world. It cleverly combines Neo-Gothic architecture with tropical and Saracenic motifs in a style which has become known as 'Bombay Gothic'.

2

Splendid Ruins

The traditional Indian interior has always been floor-orientated as in Japan. Western furniture is an acquired taste in India. There is scarcely an Indian today, no matter how Western educated or widely travelled, who is not perfectly comfortable sitting cross-legged on a floor or even sleeping on it in a pinch, and rising the next morning with no ill effects.

James Ivory

Splendid Ruins

Ever since independence, India has been searching for a renewed sense of national identity. As a result of India's years of colonial rule, Indians have become wary of European-style progress and modernization. Under the British Raj, the customs and traditions of the people were polluted by the mimicry of European culture. Yet now that India has finally broken free from colonialism it does not really know which way to turn.

Although in many ways India appears to be reverting to the traditional beliefs and attitudes of its rich, multifaceted past, it is forced to combine these with the reality of social and technological change. Modern India is certainly not rejecting all contemporary Western values outright; rather, as a new nation it is trying to establish the priorities that will forge its future.

One European value that has recently surfaced in India is the concept of restoration and renovation. India's countryside is littered with ruins, countless relics, in various states of deterioration, of its complex and extraordinary history. Yet until recently nothing was being done to preserve these magnificent examples of India's rich architectural heritage. The majority of Indians saw no value in these remnants of a glorious past because it is considered a greater virtue to build a new building than to repair an old one.

However, despite the apparent disregard for ancient buildings, a remarkable number of constructions have survived in varying states of repair. India offers immense potential for renovation and restoration of historic ruins on a vast scale. These sites also offer an opportunity to revive and put into practice a host of building skills that would otherwise, perhaps, be lost forever. The interiors of these projects offer the chance to commission work from village craftsmen.

The advent of restoration in India has largely been spearheaded by Europeans. In a bizarre cycle of influence, the *Feringi*, foreigners who were once responsible for the near-destruction of India's cultural fibre, are now instrumental in its revival. The few examples of sensitive renovation, initiated by a handful of people, are serving as role models in teaching by example how criteria of commercial and financial viability can be successfully combined with cultural awareness and tradition. Village arts and crafts and traditional building materials and skills are being used side by side with modern technology, proving that India's heritage can be taken into the modern world without having to be distorted to the point where it becomes unrecognizable.

In the following pages we look at two projects recently completed in Rajasthan. One of them, Neemrana Fort Palace, is of particular significance because of the sheer scale of the project, because it champions the use of local crafts and skills and because out of a ruin has grown a commercially successful enterprise that is both thoroughly modern and thoroughly Indian.

Neemrana Fort Palace

Legend has it that the fierce warriors of Rajasthan, the Rajputs, who in their self-perceived superiority over other warriors could not and did not consider themselves 'born of a woman', believed themselves to be direct descendants of the sun and moon, or, in the case of the Chauhan clan, which ruled over Rajasthan from 700 AD, from the holy 'fire pit' of Mount Abu. However, even this was not enough to hold back the wave of Muslim invasions. The Rajput dynasty of the Chauhan clan that had ruled from Ajmer and Delhi was defeated and driven to the southwest to the smaller kingdom of Rathd. It was here in 1464, in this new Chauhan capital of Neemrana, that Raja (king) Rajdeo built a formidable fort-palace on a picturesque plateau overlooking the town.

Rajdeo's descendants inhabited the building until 1947 when Maharaja Rajandra Singh, in the face of the abolition of princely privileges following independence, decided to abandon the palace in favour of a more modest house elsewhere in the town. The building was vandalized, and time and Nature further contributed to its deterioration. Salvation came with the arrival of Aman Nath and Francis Wacziarg. Aman Nath, an art historian born and educated in New Delhi, and Francis Wacziarg, a Frenchman, have both written extensively on the arts, crafts and culture of Rajasthan. As well as promoting craft traditions they have participated in the preservation and renovation of neglected buildings.

Nath and Wacziarg's decision to restore Neemrana Fort Palace was not taken lightly. They bought the palace and convinced O.P. Jain and Lekha Poddar to join them in their enormous project. O.P. Jain, who specializes in furniture restoration, travelled all over northern India to find suitable doors, windows and old accessories for the palace, while Lekha Poddar travelled with Aman Nath to secure the necessary hand-printed textiles that seemed a natural choice for the interior decoration. It was decided to transform the palace into a hotel and today it has the distinction of being India's oldest heritage hotel.

Basic floor plans were established from the existing fabric of the building, but in truth the palace owes its present condition to the quality of traditional skills possessed by the stone masons employed on the project. With little historical information about the palace, common sense rooted in tradition was all that guided them.

The interior decoration emphasizes the traditional Indian style: lots of floor cushions and daybeds and a smattering of antiques. All the ingredients are indigenous to India, yet the effect is very contemporary.

The product of all this careful consideration and attention to detail is an unqualified success: visually, culturally, and financially. Every weekend the fort-palace is filled by people eager to escape the noise and pollution of Delhi, but Neemrana's greatest success is as a role model for other renovation projects.

Emptiness is infinitely satisfying to the
human mind. Art and architecture are
simply the concrete externalizations of our
attempts to understand that void.
Charles Correa

Sophisticated and refined, these are
interiors that create mood and beauty by
clever use of the simplest ingredients.

Francis Wacziarg

Udaipur Lake House

When Shah Jahan took flight in 1623 from the forces of his father, Jahangir, in a succession struggle for the throne of the Mughal Empire, he chose to spend his exile on the island of Jag Mandir in the middle of the lake at Udaipur. No stranger to beauty, this aesthete, who would later sit on the Mughal throne and build the Taj Mahal, would undoubtedly have been charmed by the magnificence of this lake-side city. Udaipur had been started by Udai Singh, head of the most senior house in Rajasthan and figurehead to all Hindus in northern India, who in 1567 found himself in flight from the conquering forces of Akbar, Shah Jahan's grandfather, who had laid siege to the Hindu's capital city at Chittor. Udaipur, named after its founder, grew to become one of India's most beautiful cities, and today is one of its star attractions.

Nearby, and ideally located on the edge of Udaipur Lake, is a house belonging to an Italian artist which has recently been renovated. This *haveli*, a mansion once owned by a wealthy merchant, is typical of many houses that are scattered throughout the towns and cities of Rajasthan.

Udaipur Lake House is a model argument for a return to simplicity and authenticity: the decoration is minimal throughout and is limited to floor cushions and day-beds, utilizing local sources such as hand-loomed fabrics from nearby villages and furniture made by the local carpenters. Mood and beauty are created by clever use of the simplest ingredients: a carefully placed terra-cotta pot, a bed on a swing in the middle of a room, block-printed textiles on cushions arranged in comfortable layers on the floor, a dowry-chest to store additional cushions and textiles set against a wall. The manner and style of day-to-day life in this house varies little from the time when Shah Jahan spent his four months on Udaipur Lake.

A key feature of the house, which is increasingly being exploited by Indian architects in contemporary domestic projects, is the easy, almost seamless transition between outdoor and indoor space. Outdoor pavilions, open to the breezes from the lake but covered from the sun, are as much part of the house as interior rooms. Transition between these areas is determined mostly by the heat; thus, at different times during the day, life moves as naturally as the sun itself between indoor and outdoor spaces. This instinctive way of living, on the floor, in migration to different spaces throughout the house, without the strict Western definitions of specific purpose for each room, is distinctly Indian.

Udaipur Lake House, in its reinvention of a lifestyle based on traditional simplicity, is completely in step with a new movement in contemporary Indian architecture; a movement that rejects inappropriate Western influences and trends. A project such as this demonstrates that renovation, utilizing an approach that is simple, appropriate and modern, can be a step towards reclaiming Indian culture.

It is quite possible that India is the
real world, and that the white man
lives in a madhouse of abstractions...
Life in India has not yet withdrawn
into the capsule of the head. It is still
the whole body that lives. No wonder
the European feels dreamlike: the
complete life of India is something of
which he merely dreams... I did not see one
European in India who really lived there.
They were all living in Europe, that is,
in a sort of bottle filled with European air.
One would surely go under without
the insulating glass wall; one would
be drowned in all the things which
we Europeans have conquered in
our imagination.

Carl Gustav Jung

PAGE 58
The second set of gate-doors to Neemrana Fort Palace would originally have guarded the entry to the accommodation quarters of the fort. Although now purely decorative, they offer an insight into the attitudes and characteristics of Indian culture. The finely painted and decorated inside edge of the doorway is in sharp contrast to the robust and rather functional brutality of the doors which were built to withstand a certain amount of abuse.

PAGES 60-61
Built as a fortified palace for the Maharaja of Neemrana in 1464 AD, this imposing fort was abandoned after Indian independence in 1947. In this spectacular piece of architectural renovation parts of the fort-palace have been left in ruin, and efforts were concentrated on particular sections of the building to enable a significant proportion of the rooms to be transformed into a small and charmingly appointed hotel.

PAGE 62
The gentle patina of time has been left untouched on the walls of this faded courtyard. An important aspect of the success of the renovation of Neemrana Fort Palace is the sensitivity shown to detail: the old and the crumbling have been allowed to co-exist with the new and freshly painted, resisting the temptation as is so often the case with restoration to make it 'better than new'.

PAGE 65
A carefully selected collection of doors, windows, chairs, tables and artefacts from all over northern India furnish the individual rooms of the fort in a manner that complements the character of each space. This particular suite, with its polished marble floor and high ceilings, is cool, serene and elegant. The furniture has been limited to a few antique prayer chairs with hand-loomed fabrics used to cover the bed and floor cushions.

PAGE 66
Neemrana Fort Palace was built by the descendants of the last ruling Hindu family of north India – the Chauhans – who ruled from Ajmer and Delhi until 1192 AD. Neemrana became their third home when the Muslims replaced them as rulers. A strong architectural feature of the fort, found on this external wall to one of the original private chambers, are the repetitive geometric forms and arches which are indicative of the mixing of Hindu and Islamic styles.

PAGE 67
This corridor, on the other side of the wall shown on page 66, was originally used by the Maharajas' wives to get in and out of their private rooms without being seen by visitors to the fort. The combination of the unexpected deep blue of the long narrow space, and the decorative effect of the daylight that enters through the elaborate stone screens or *jali*, is another example of the secret spaces that have survived the renovation of the fort.

PAGES 68-69
The focal meeting place of the fort is an outdoor area set high on an exterior corner which looks out to the village below. The steps leading to the roof and the balcony through the cutout in the wall, offer a spectacular view of the desert which stretches out from the outskirts of the village. In the morning, tables are set for breakfast while the desert chill is still in the air.

PAGES 70-71
The furniture for most of the suites was chosen by O.P. Jain, who specializes in furniture restoration. The approach to the interior decoration of the fort emphasizes simplicity and suitability. A pre-renovation photograph hangs in each room to remind guests of the enormity of the task undertaken. The portrait on the easel is of the Maharaja when he still occupied the fort.

PAGE 73
Bathrooms at Neemrana are an architectural delight. Each one is completely different and they have been squeezed into the most unusual and unlikely places. This one, which belongs to the suite shown on page 65, is one of the grander bathrooms – it has a very high ceiling, a marble floor, an antique Rajasthani timber door to the linen-closet, and the space offered by most normal hotel rooms.

PAGE 74
This former wealthy merchant's house on the edge of Udaipur Lake has been restored by an Italian artist who lives in India for part of each year. This renovation project, not unlike the commitment to Neemrana Fort Palace but on a smaller scale, was undertaken to restore the house to a habitable condition. Unusually, the rains had not come when this photograph was taken and, as a result, all the steps are visible.

PAGE 76-77 The hedged courtyard garden is the true living-room of this house. Planted with mango trees and extending into the lake so that the water laps against the retaining wall, entertaining takes place in the shade of the arched cupolas at the water-side end of the garden. In the heat of a Rajasthani summer, this is an ideal place to enjoy the view of the lake and be cooled by gentle winds coming off the water.

PAGE 78
With the benefit of an artist's eye, the renovation of the house was tackled with a regard for simplicity and appropriateness. Details, such as the patches of blue paint, accentuate the architectural design and reinforce the natural sense of colour that is so pervasive in India.

PAGE 79
Visitors to this house remark on its similarity to houses in the Mediterranean, especially those of Morocco and Turkey, and this is not pure coincidence; the conquering influence of Islam drew a cultural band from northern India to the Atlantic coast of Morocco. Since these places share more or less the same latitude they also have, apart from a common cultural link, similar climatic conditions.

PAGE 80
This lakeside pavilion, the venue for most entertaining, encapsulates the main aspects of Indian culture that have begun to resurface in the wake of colonial rule: an informal use of space, a return to the patronage of village crafts, such as weaving (in this case hand-woven fabrics cover the cushions), and a less distinct separation of interior and exterior space.

3

Indigenous Skills

The challenge for the modern architect is
the same as the challenge for all of us in
our lives: to make out of the ordinary
something out-of-the-ordinary.

Patrick Nuttgens

Indigenous Skills

For centuries the skills of India's craftsmen were admired and coveted the world over. Without India's building repertoire, particularly in stone, the grandeur and magnificence of monuments such as the Taj Mahal would never have been achieved. Stone masonry found its earliest expression in the construction and decoration of temples. Masons were protected and encouraged by powerful guilds and guided by the early sacred texts on art and architecture, such as the *Mayamatha* and the *Shilpashastra*, which set out requirements for sculpting technique as well as those for colour, texture and maturity of stone.

Until the twentieth century, when concrete was introduced as a convenient building material, stone and mud bricks had been the preferred medium. But in a hurry to join the 'modern' world, the traditional materials were abandoned and concrete was adopted as the material with which the new India would build its future. Concrete was light, technologically advanced, versatile and, most importantly, it was what the West was using. In the space of five decades, the highly developed skills of building in stone and mortar were dropped in favour of 'the wheel barrow, two shovels and a concrete mixer'. Very rapidly, India's most significant achievement – that of unparalleled cultural continuity – was threatened by a material inferior in durability and aesthetics and with which the people had no affinity. Yet it was not just the skill of building in stone that was threatened by the advent of concrete. Building in mud bricks, a technique developed in the northwestern states of India before the dawn of Christianity, was also challenged by the 'efficiency' of concrete.

Today, the failure of concrete as a suitable building material for India is becoming increasingly evident. Many of India's architects are beginning to refocus their thinking and are exploring opportunities of working with traditional skills in a contemporary way.

Two projects using mud and two projects using stone and mortar, shown on the following pages, are examples of this current movement in architecture. Nimish Patel, the architect behind the two projects that utilize traditional stone masonry, is realistic enough to understand that these few isolated applications are only relevant in the sense that they may spark a greater movement. As he says, 'unless conservation of our cultural heritage becomes a way of life for the people there is very little chance for it to gain momentum... and momentum is the only way to imbue the nation with these new values'.

Mud Architecture

Mandawa Desert Camp

Indian tribal architecture has continued virtually unaltered for thousands of years. The annual ornamentation of mud huts has been a form of worship and homage to the gods since the times of pre-Hindu animist faiths when it was believed that specific diagrams had the power to contain and direct the supernatural. The ancient Sanskrit works on Indian painting, for instance, describe the worship of the sun god through the drawing of an eight-petalled lotus flower. The materials and techniques traditionally handed down from mother to daughter are charged with symbolic meaning. By depicting the gods they are summoning them to enter the house. Daughters of the villages practise painting from the age of four and by the time they reach their teens they are fluent in the forms that express their spiritual expectations. This tradition of surrounding the doors and windows of mud houses with decorative painting is still carried out throughout the villages of India in an annual ritual of renewal. The purpose is not only decorative but also symbolic of a sacred and protective role and reveals the deeper meaning underlying the mud structures of the village.

Mandawa Desert Camp, a resort hotel developed by Revathi and Vasant Kamath, a husband and wife architectural team based in Delhi, was designed to recreate the atmosphere and incorporate the images, forms and spaces of a typical village of rural Rajasthan. Yet this Desert Camp is not a straight copy of a Rajasthani village: in balance with the ethnic authenticity of the design, Mandawa also incorporates the contemporary conveniences and luxuries that today's five-star guest demands. Indeed, it is this very juxtaposition of Indian traditions and Western considerations that makes Mandawa so successful.

The Kamaths have emerged as India's leading protagonists of mud architecture and this is one of their most highly acclaimed projects. It is an example of a growing practice among India's architects to produce contemporary work in a traditional idiom, and contribute to post-independence India's strong and recognizable cultural identity.

Local craftsmen were employed by the Kamaths to construct the resort: village carpenters made the furniture, local masons built the structures and the women from the villages hand-plastered and decorated the walls with mouldings, relief-work, embedded mirrors and symbolic tribal painting. Sun-dried bricks were made from the bed of a dried-out water tank adjacent to the site; thatch was created from grass growing on the property itself, and the stone for the foundations, sills, lintels, brackets and roofing came from a nearby village. As contemporary comforts are seamlessly combined with traditional Indian finishes, the visitor to Mandawa Desert Camp is enveloped by a richness of textures, colours and decorative details that evoke the symbolism of an ancient tribal village and offer a unique Indian experience.

When we talk of building in mud, I don't know why we term it 'alternative' building. The natural way is to build with mud, stone, timber, thatch and so-called bio-materials. I work with these materials because they are beautiful and powerful. That, to me, is justification enough. It is most wonderful to know that when a building has outlived its life, it can return to the earth. When you work with mud and hand plaster the walls, it is like forming an external skin; it is as if every bit of the building embodies the human spirit, the cyclic care of the building being a part of the act of living.

Revathi Kamath

Mapu's Farm

As an introduction to the rich and continuous traditions of rural India, Mandawa Desert Camp plays an important role. It recreates a traditional village with the techniques that would have been used for centuries, thereby awakening an awareness and an appreciation of indigenous skills. For mud to be accepted as anything other than a surviving relic, however, its application must extend beyond the traditional village. Indeed, like renovation, mud will only earn a new image when it establishes a new frame of reference and is used in a contemporary fashion.

There is no better example of this than in the farmhouse belonging to Martand Singh and the textile designer Rakesh Thakore. Set in a quiet rural area on the outskirts of Delhi, the house is a simple, minimally designed, modern retreat. Strictly speaking, the structure is not an example of traditional mud architecture – it is actually built in stone – but mud has been rendered over the stone in a traditional manner. Applied annually, by hand, in sweeping circular motions, by women from a local village, the mud render on the exterior walls simply washes away under the relentless deluge of the monsoon, and with the onset of dry weather the walls are re-rendered. This method is not only practical, it is also completely in step with Hindu beliefs concerning the cyclical nature of life. Inside, mud is used as a natural backdrop to a carefully chosen selection of furniture, artefacts and building materials.

In this contemporary setting, the expansive stretches of mud walls work particularly well with the use of natural colours, materials and details in the house. The floors are made of Khota stone, a grey, green stone that is found in abundance throughout northern India. Polished everyday with rags soaked in oil, the floor will improve with time as the lustre and depth of colour progresses towards a dark green, almost black, sombre hue.

Decoration relies on basic ingredients: large white terracotta pots, floor cushions made from block-printed cottons, stone slabs as tabletops, candles in large antique oil lamps and earthenware bowls filled with flower petals which are arranged tastefully throughout the house. The manner in which these ingredients of Indian culture have been used to create a contemporary environment is a suitable and apt approach, considering the background of the two owners.

Martand Singh is a designer and writer whose own nickname – Mapu – is a badge of respect, a term of general endearment that he has earned from India's cultural community. Mapu was instrumental in the establishment of INTACH, the Indian National Trust for the Arts and Cultural Heritage, a nationwide organization committed to the preservation of India's cultural heritage, which seeks to revive traditional skills and endow them with a relevancy in today's world.

I do not see mud architecture as a symbol of poverty, nor would I like to use mud to express images of high technology, as some architects are attempting to do. I see potential in its use as a material to continue the tradition of architectural skills that exist, and thereby ensure a continuity of traditional aesthetic sensibilities and knowledge.

Revathi Kamath

Building in Stone

Amber Haveli and the Singh House

Amber is one of the most magnificent cities in Rajasthan. Situated in a narrow gorge and flanked by a majestic fort palace, it was the capital of the Kachakawa clan of Rajputs for six centuries (1135 – 1727 AD) until Jai Singh II built the city of Jaipur, less than an hour's drive away. Today, tourists come to visit the fort palace, but away from the tour buses there is another Amber where John Singh, a Jaipur businessman and proponent of the need to conserve India's heritage, has initiated a privately funded project to rebuild one of the many ruined *havelis* (eighteenth-century merchants' houses).

The house was restored using the traditional Rajasthani stone and mortar technique: walls are built of carefully stacked stones and then bonded and sealed with a lime mortar. The mortar thus acts as both render and mortar. The photograph on page 106 shows the construction before the lime render was applied. The secret of this ancient construction technique lies with the lime mortar. All over India there are temples and palaces built using the stone and mortar technique which, despite 700 or more years of eventful history and an unsympathetic climate, have walls that are as smooth as marble. Research has revealed that the lime has to go through a fermentation process which sounds more like mixing an exotic drink than preparing a building material: lime is thrown into a rudimentary outdoor tank, water is added and the mixture left to ferment in the heat of the day, with more

water added intermittently together with citrus juices, crushed sea shells, and stone dust from pink sandstone or white marble. As a result of the fermentation the lime mortar, once applied, sets as hard and strong as the stone itself.

It is on interior walls that the refinement of these traditional building skills really comes to the fore. As successive layers of lime have a chance to harden, the last coatings are trowelled on in increasingly finer layers and as they begin to set the walls are polished with wet rags. These walls, which by this stage already have a finish similar to that of expensive writing paper, once sufficiently dry are buffed further to the equivalent finish of the finest porcelain. Only then are the walls decorated.

As a result of the lessons learned in renovating the *haveli* in Amber, John Singh decided to apply the stone and mortar technique to a new house, choosing the farmhouse that he was building on the outskirts of Jaipur. The house, the result of collaboration between the Singhs, their architect Nimish Patel and the local craftsmen and builders, is built around a courtyard open on one side to the garden. In this way, the design reflects the indoor/outdoor nature of the Indian way of life. Detailing, such as the curved stone *jali* for the windows, the Karoli stone pillars, the choice of local marble and yellow and pink sandstone for the floor, shows the owners' and architects' commitment to the use of traditional skills and materials in a contemporary setting.

The act of practising architecture in
India today is dominated by the desire
to invent authenticity.

Romi Khosla

PAGE 86

A detail of the tribal decoration on the mud walls at Mandawa Desert Camp, Rajasthan. An inspiring example of traditional skills executed in contemporary architecture, materials, processes and traditions. Designed by architects Revathi and Vasant Kamath, the Desert Camp recreates the atmosphere of a village in the Shekawati region of Rajasthan.

PAGES 88-89

An eye-catching bulbous wall made from moulded terracotta pots is a tribute to the model of the potter's house it surrounds. Originally conceived as a windbreak, its randomly lumpy form is accentuated by the smoother lines of the house. The use of terracotta pots as a building ingredient is a feature of traditional Rajasthani architecture.

PAGE 90

A typical hut (housing a suite) at Mandawa Desert Camp is based on the traditional forms and spaces of a village house of the Shekawati region of Rajasthan. The huts are designed to represent the homes of the village farmer, potter and weaver in a manner that visitors can experience and comprehend.

PAGES 92-93

Although the spatial sequence and architectural elements of the huts are based on the house forms of the weaver, potter and farmer, the accommodation plan of each hut has taken full account of the needs and requirements of five-star tourists. Without sacrificing authenticity, these interiors are fully equipped with modern, beautifully-crafted stone bathrooms and exceptional amounts of storage space.

PAGES 94-95

Local masons built the structures at Mandawa Desert Camp using sun-dried mud bricks and the women from neighbouring villages hand-plastered and finished the walls with traditional mouldings, relief detailing and embedded mirror-work.

PAGE 96

Mandawa Desert Camp combines a responsibility towards traditional skills and knowledge with a modern sense of practical simplicity, which has become the emerging signature of the Indian architect.

PAGE 98

The construction and decoration of Mapu's farm is simple and authentic; twin cutouts on either side of the staircase reinforce the mathematical symmetry characteristic of India's architectural heritage. Walls rendered in mud contrast with the occasional whitewashed interior wall; floors are of Khota stone; timber furniture is by local craftsmen; and decorative pots are by artist friends. (The hanging lamp is a rice paper balloon by Japanese sculptor Isamu Noguchi.)

PAGES 100-101

A covered outdoor entertaining area reflects the ingredients of life in India: weaving, stone, pottery, colour and mud, which, when combined as successfully as they are in this instance, define the meaning of an emerging contemporary Indian style.

PAGE 103
Afternoon light accentuates the attractive patina of traditional mud render. Renewed annually by women from a nearby village, the mud is applied by hand and smeared in a sweeping circular motion creating a distinctive texture and colour. This traditional technique helps to accentuate form and space, and in a truly modern sense reduces the need for elaborate decoration.

PAGE 104
The design of this house is a diamond shape, where the convergence point at one end is the entrance, and at the other, the courtyard shrine. The front of the house is essentially a wedge shape and the entrance as shown is placed at the point where the two walls converge. As an architectural device this is the most appropriate place for a formal entry and, importantly, it places the entrance in a direct line with the axis of the courtyard at the rear of the house.

PAGE 105
Placed at a 45-degree angle to the converging courtyard walls, the shrine in the courtyard is, appropriately, the internal focal-point of the house. The central status of spirituality in life is thus reinforced by the architecture. Interestingly, the composition and adornment of the shrine does not differ from ingredients used throughout the house.

PAGE 106 All over northern India, the monumental palaces, temples, and tombs of an impressive architectural legacy have survived, some virtually intact, because of the way they were constructed. These structures would surely have crumbled if it had not been for the extraordinary skills of the lime renderers who sealed each building with a protective coating that in some cases has lasted for 800 years. This *hareli* (mansion), situated in the ancient city of Amber in Rajasthan, was entirely rebuilt using these traditional skills. This photograph shows the structure just before it was lime-rendered.

PAGES 108-109
Inspired by the success of his project to renovate the *hareli* in Amber, John Singh decided to build his own house using traditional Rajasthani methods and materials. The house is a triumph of collaboration between the architects, the owners and the builders. Architecture by process rather than by design, resulting in an unmistakably Indian, yet thoroughly modern building.

PAGE 110
Influenced by Sri Lankan architect Geoffrey Bawa and Egyptian architect Hassan Fathy, the Singhs were particularly concerned about the correct use of materials in relation to the harsh climate. In its composition, the house is almost entirely constructed of local stone and lime mortar.

PAGES 112-113
Designed with a strong commitment to the concept of indoor and outdoor space, the Singhs' farmhouse features a courtyard that acts as a continuation of the interior living area. Bordered by walls pierced by stone *jali* and decorated in chevron-patterned Jaipur blue pottery tiles, the courtyard incorporates a fountain with both still and running water.

PAGES 114-115
A typical villager's daybed, primitive sculptures from Orissa, and a repetitive rhythm of Mughal arch-shaped cutouts are the only ornaments that enhance the stylishly simple swimming pool. Utilizing an ancient system, the pool is kept clean without the use of any chemicals. It acts as a reservoir for the orchard irrigation system, thus ensuring the water in the pool is constantly renewed.

4

A Natural
Sense of Colour

Colour adds to the total experience of
architecture; it can make space infinite.

Le Corbusier

A Natural Sense of Colour

Colour has played a significant role in Indian culture for more than 3,000 years, and in the country's trade with other civilizations. Early visitors to India were overwhelmed by the nature of the colours they encountered in the fabrics, partly because there are more than 300 dye plants that are indigenous to the subcontinent. But the skill of the craftsmen or *rangrez* (a dyer: rang = colour, rez = to pour) was not only dependent on the variety of dyes available. They also knew about mordants (usually in the form of metal salts) which would fix the colour. The discovery of colourfast dyes was simultaneous with the development of cotton weaving. Cotton, a vegetable fibre, would only accept vegetable-based dyes in the same way as animal-based fibres, such as wool and silk, with the aid of mordants. It was in this way that the craftsmen could get locally woven cotton to accept their extraordinary repertoire of colours. The brilliantly coloured cotton rapidly became a sought-after commodity in the ancient world.

Colour is an integral part of all facets of life in India – social status, religion and celebration. It was used by the invading Aryans to underpin the caste system. Each *varna*, the Sanskrit word that came to mean class, had its distinguishing colour: white for *brahmins* (priests), red for *kshatriyas* (warriors), brown for *vaishyas* (merchants) and black for *shudras* (menial workers). Colour is used to convey meaning in a country of many languages and poor levels of literacy, for example saffron is the colour of the *sadhus* (sages).

Nothing demonstrates more spectacularly how colour is a part of the Indian soul than *Holi*, the Festival of Spring. In the weeks prior to the lively two-day celebration, the village, town and city streets are lined with carts displaying beautifully arranged mounds of brightly coloured powder. During the festival all social hierarchy is forgotten and in a frenzied carnival atmosphere of dancing and drum-playing people are smeared in the coloured powder and doused by coloured water. For days afterwards it is not unusual to come across taxi-drivers with pink and orange hair, shopkeepers with yellow and green faces or waiters with blue necks.

Holi is just one example of how colour and religion are joined together in India. Another is in the depiction of the blue god, Krishna, the god of love. His youthful pranks and heroic acts have endeared him to the Indian people. Wherever you go you find the unmistakable indigo of Krishna's skin: as a fat blue baby stealing butter-balls out of the kitchen, a naughty blue teenager hiding the clothes of the women bathing in the river or a robust blue adult winning battles and conquering hearts. Indigo is one of the few dyes which do not need a mordant. The strength and fastness of its colour led to a thriving trade in indigo between India and the West and it would seem more than pure coincidence that the colour of the strongest dye is also the colour of the most popular god.

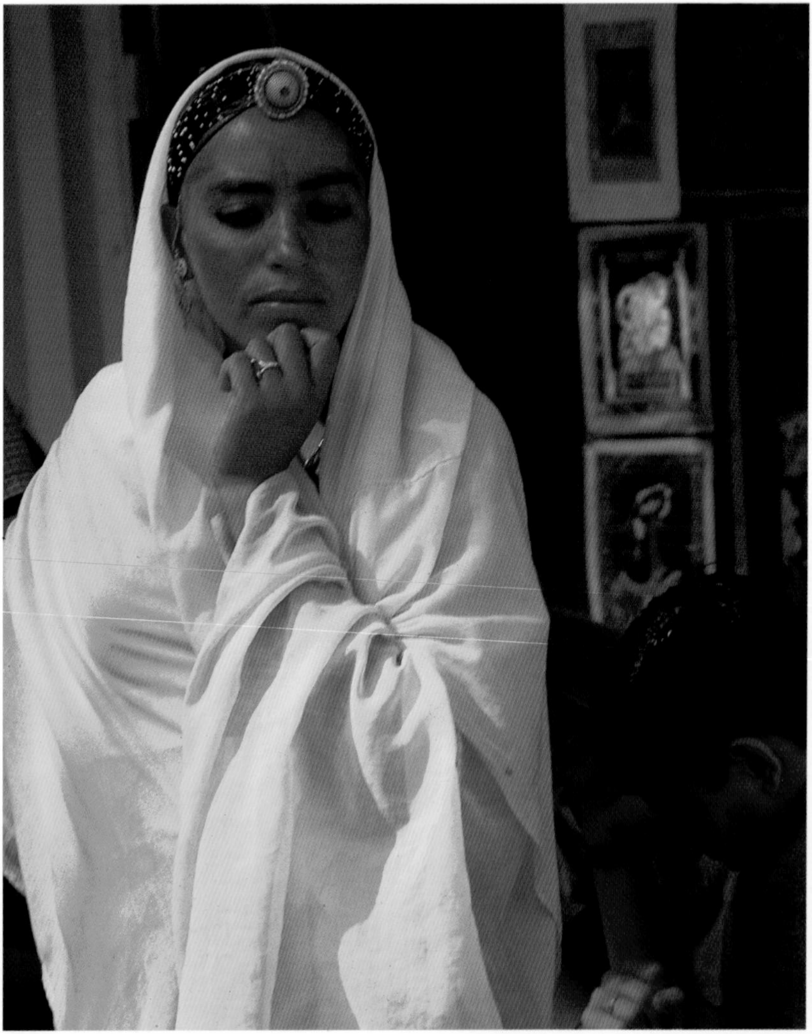

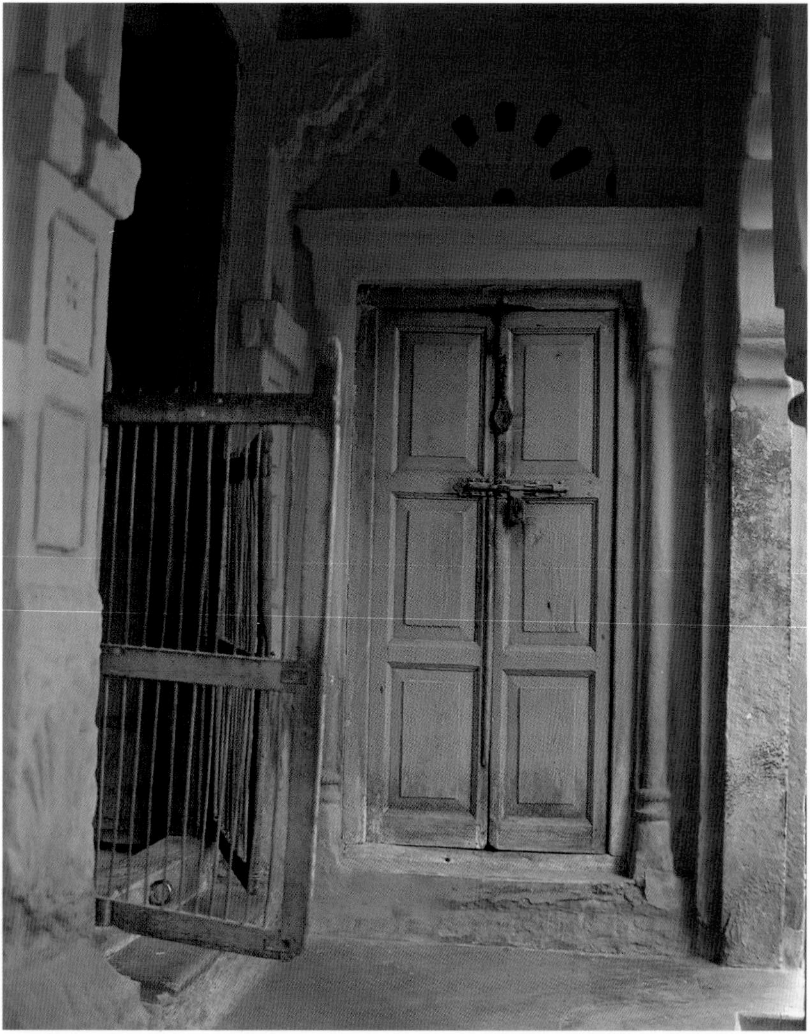

Pink is the navy blue of India.

Diana Vreeland

PAGE 120
A Rajput merchant in the city of Jodhpur. This simple portrait reveals a lot about the natural sense of colour that is pervasive in India. People in India understand inherently how to wear colour. The orange of this man's orange turban is vividly brought to life by the fact that he wears no other colour but white.

PAGES 122-123
One of the most extraordinary places in Rajasthan is the town of Jodhpur, where the doors, walls, steps and windows are painted in various shades of blue. Because the effect of this colour is so startling, photographs of the town are often thought to have been created by some sort of trick photography.

PAGES 124-125
Blue is the colour used to distinguish the Brahmin (educated) caste and in its application, particularly en masse as in this example, the colour has a serene authority which is entirely in keeping with its context. Interestingly, however, in ancient Vedic times white was the designated colour for the Brahmin. An explanation for the change to blue perhaps lies in the growing popularity of the Lord Krishna who is always depicted in indigo.

PAGE 126
Saris and *odhnis*, still the essential component of the wardrobe for most Indian women, are passed down from generation to generation. Cloth is considered a commodity. Its worth is related to the complexity of the weave, the cost of the ingredients, and the hours of work that went into creating it. Preference for colour is dictated not only by personal choice, but also by geography: brighter, more saturated colours are more commonly seen in the north, while softer pastel shades tend to be the preferred choice in the south.

PAGE 127
In India colour extends beyond outward appearances. Indeed, in Hindi the word *raga* means both 'mood' and 'dye'. Colours are a projection of the mood evoked by changing seasons. Yellow, for instance, is the colour of spring, of fields of marigolds, and young mango blossoms.

PAGES 128-129
In the weeks and days leading up to *Holi*, affectionately known as the Festival of Colour, bags of brightly coloured powder are sold by street vendors to the population who throw it at each other on the actual day. In this instance, the vendor understands the impact that the display of just one colour can have: neat architectural mounds of red summon the eye from a distance.

PAGES 130 AND 131
Since the Aryan age, with its strictly stratified social system, red has also been the colour of the warrior class – the *kshatriya*. Thus it is appropriate that in Rajasthan, home of one of the proudest and fiercest fighting heritages in India, red should be a popular choice for turbans. Certain shades, however, have a hierarchical meaning. For instance, Imperial Red is recognized as being the 'privilege of princes'.

PAGES 132-133
Photographed late in the day, the soft light produced by the afternoon sun in the Rajasthani town of Jodhpur has turned a typical blue-painted wall almost purple; a colourful sight when contrasted with the green shutters. Almost shocking in their intensity, these fluorescent hues enliven the dark narrow streets in which these houses can be found.

PAGES 134-135
Each year millions of roses are sold in the streets and temples of India. In Ajmer, the rose-scented streets lead to one of India's most important places of pilgrimage for Muslims – the Dargah tomb of the Sufi saint Khawaja Muin-udin Chishti. Every day, rose sellers line the streets and alleyways, and red and pink roses are piled high on the tomb.

PAGES 136 AND 137
Two arbitrarily chosen houses in Jodhpur demonstrate the powerful use of colour in India. In nearly every city the same colours and combinations of colours constantly re-occur as a response to tradition and intuition.

PAGES 138-139
Turbans are the equivalent of ties in the West: pieces of decorative fabric that, in terms of choice of colour and in the manner in which they are tied, reveal a lot about the character and personality of the individual. This herdsman at the Pushkar Camel Fair is a particularly robust character and he has a turban to match.

PAGES 140-141
With over 300 indigenous dye-yielding plants, India was one of the first civilizations to master dye technology. This, combined with the early development of weaving skills in cotton, led village craftsmen to produced cotton textiles in such seductive shades that they soon became a highly-prized commodity in the ancient Mediterranean civilizations of Greece, Rome and Egypt.

PAGES 142
In India colour is everywhere: even the most ramshackle shutter, door or window does not escape decoration. Unlike in the West, buildings do not have to be renovated before they warrant a coat of paint. Perfection is not the aim, but rather to give every aspect of life as much colour as possible.

PAGE 143
A recently painted Brahmin house in the old town of Jodhpur serves as a splendid backdrop for the sacred cow that wanders freely through the streets. Blue and white, the two colours that at different times in India's history have been representative of the Brahmin caste, are combined in one composition.

PAGE 144
In India pink is ubiquitous and every imaginable shade of magenta is worn, particularly in Rajasthan. Against his dark eyes and skin, this man's pink turban looks decidedly flattering and appropriate.

PAGES 146-147
Established in 1875, Mayo College in Ajmer, Rajasthan, is known as the 'Eton of India'. Each year at graduation, the boys assemble dressed in traditional uniform. Wearing the turban colour of their House, they create a colourful collage as they wait anxiously for their names to be called.

5

Cultural
Ingredients

I try and draw on existent, if tenuous, craft
techniques and skills and extend
them into a contemporary context.
I suppose it is essentially about new
ways of looking at the familiar.

Asha Sarabhai

Cultural Ingredients

Throughout history, India has been considered a mythical land of fabulous riches. Alexander the Great was lured by fanciful descriptions of 'giant gold digging ants who laboured in gold strewn deserts'. But the young general never reached the Gangetic plain and would never discover that the legend of India's wealth was, indeed, no myth. And all these riches were contained within what is described in Hindu mythology as 'the wisdom of the hand'. Hindus so prized the ability to create that they believed that the 'hands that created' were divinely guided and that creativity and religion were inseparable. According to Hindu mythology, Lord Vishnu, the solar deity, was the 'divine weaver' who is said to have woven the rays of the sun into a garment for himself. Similarly, Brahma, having made man from a clay vessel was the first potter.

This craft tradition was thus the very foundation on which India's wealth and stability had stood since time immemorial. Yet this foundation was almost destroyed by the coming of the Industrial Revolution in Europe. What was the relevance, India's colonial overlords asked, of handiwork in an age when machines could make things faster, cheaper and better?

The only man, it seemed, who had an answer to this challenge from the industrialized West was *Mahatma* (Great Souled One) Gandhi. Early in the struggle for independence Gandhi emerged with an overriding concern for the needs and welfare of the masses. For Gandhi it was essential for the new India to emerge from an understanding of indigenous traditions and values, and so he turned back to the craft traditions of the village as a means of defining India's strengths and culture. When violent clashes occurred as a result of one of his campaigns of civil disobedience, Gandhi responded by retreating to his *ashram* and his spinning wheel. Slowly and laboriously he would spin his own yarn and weave his own cloth (*khadi*) and during this process he would contemplate the best course for him and his followers to take towards independence. So convinced was Gandhi of the power of handicrafts that the spinning wheel became the symbol of the Congress Party and each member's dues were established at 2,000 yards of handspun yarn a month. Gandhi believed that daily spinning would bring India's leaders into closer touch with peasant life and enhance the dignity of labour in the minds of Indian intellectuals who had never done a day's physical work in their lives.

As a result handicrafts achieved a higher status in newly independent India. Gandhi had set an example for the entire nation. In today's India a new generation of designers is seeking to make ancient skills viable in a modern context through employing unfamiliar concepts of design and marketing. Working with India's village artisans, designers in fields as diverse as rug-making, ceramics, clothing, accessories and pottery are producing items of considerable originality and extraordinary beauty.

Kora
Asha Sarabhai

India produces the largest variety of textiles in the world: silks, cottons, calicos, jutes, rayons, muslins and wools that are dyed, vat-dyed, block-printed, quilted, brocaded, embroidered, *Ikat*-woven, double *Ikat*-woven, mirror-clad, metal-clad, weft-faced and knotted to create a vast kaleidoscope of creative expressions in fabric. Amongst this ocean of choice, the *Kora* fabrics of Asha Sarabhai stand out like a haven of calm in a sea of colour and ornamentation.

Kora is the Hindi word for loom-state, that is cotton yarn before it is bleached or dyed, and forms the foundation of Asha Sarabhai's textile designs. Her preference for this natural material is not so much a rejection of colour, as a concern for the weave of the cloth which, feels Sarabhai, recedes into the background when it is dyed. Influenced by modern art, she has sought to develop an aesthetic that is both indigenous to India and contemporary in design, creating products that reveal real Indian culture without resorting to visual clichés.

To achieve this Sarabhai has resorted to a minimalist or reductive approach to design, abandoning the bright or obvious colours of India in favour of subtle hues, or no colour at all, and dropping the popular decorative approaches of the hand-loom, such as block printing or tie-dyeing, in favour of the texture of the cloth itself. This is not a rejection of Indian heritage or tradi-

tion; indeed it is quite the opposite. 'It is', she says, 'about drawing on existing craft techniques and skills and extending them into a contemporary context... about new ways of looking at the familiar.' The essence of Indian textiles, for her, is craftsmanship and, in particular, the specialized skills of the village weavers: for Sarabhai the true identity of Indian fabric lies deeper than surface decoration; there is a notion of depth and meaning which mirrors traditional Hindu mythology.

To reflect her dedication to the weavers craft her vocabulary of fabric design includes pleating, folding and bunching, whereby the fabric is used to decorate itself. The practice of pleating as a decorative device for textiles has a historic pedigree. At the start of the century Mario Fortuny, the famous Venetian inventor, artist and aristocrat, made a name the world over for his extraordinarily beautiful pleated silks. In recent times Issey Miyake, the Japanese fashion designer, has picked up where Fortuny left off, introducing unique surface and texture effects on newly developed synthetic materials to produce a modern variation of Fortuny's theme. Miyake's garments, in common with Sarabhai's designs, rely on structure and texture of the cloth rather than decorative effect. Sarabhai has worked with Miyake and undoubtedly they have been influenced by each other's designs.

Jaipur Blue Pottery

Kripal Singh

Blue-glaze pottery was first introduced to India in the sixteenth century by Babur, the first Mughal conqueror of Hindustan. Babur, a Mongol from the ancient central Asian territory of Transoxania, was a direct descendant of the infamous and merciless conqueror Timur 'the lame' (or 'Tamerlane') who would leave his capital of Samarkand, the beautiful city of 'blue tiled' buildings, on his far-reaching, cruel and bloody conquests. As spoils of war, Timur soon collected a community of craftsmen who were employed to work on his impressive tomb, the *Gur Amir*, which became renowned thoughout the world for its beautiful dome.

The craftsmen who decorated the *Gur Amir* had learned to combine Chinese glazing technology with Persian decorative arts. This technique travelled with Babur to Hindustan where it was introduced to the craftsmen of India. Blue pottery became a fixed ingredient of Mughal culture, where glazed tiles were used to decorate mosques, tombs and palaces, mimicking the beloved effigies in central Asia. The use and scope of this Mughal tradition increased with each subsequent ruler of the Mughal empire until inexplicably its use ceased altogether. In the words of Kripal Singh, the man widely credited with the modern resurrection of this craft: 'The early craftsmen went to great lengths to keep the whole process as a heavily guarded secret. They deliberately confused and discouraged other potters just to maintain their dominance and managed, instead, to create problems for themselves. Within a very short period blue pottery just started to vanish.'

For years Kripal Singh travelled extensively to the United States, Europe, Mexico, Canada, Iran and Thailand, to try to put the pieces of 'the jigsaw puzzle' together. His gritty determination and persistence eventually led to success. Today, Jaipur Blue pottery is once again in great demand. Attracted by the same beauty, no doubt, that caught the eyes of Timur, Babur, Shah Jahan and Jai Singh, the distinct signature of Kripal Singh's blue-glazed pottery is also in demand in export markets such as the United States, Great Britain, France and Japan. Completely in step with modern times the handmade quality of the work serves to distinguish it from manufactured bowls and plates and reinforces its status as an object of instrinsic value. Fortunately for posterity's sake, Kripal Singh is no longer the only person producing blue and white glazed ware. He has trained enough apprentices over the years to ensure the survival, this time, of this well-travelled, cosmopolitan, creative tradition.

Ikat

Rakesh Thakore

Together with opium. *Ikat* is historically one of India's most successful exports to Asia. Both commodities were used as part of a system of international barter by the colonial powers. Opium from India was used by the British to acquire tea and silk in China for sale in Britain. The Dutch East India Company's equivalent to opium was *Ikat*. These exquisite cotton and silk textiles, woven by villagers in Gujarat, Orissa and Andhra Pradesh, were purchased at little cost by the Dutch traders who called on the north-west ports of India and then transported the cloth to Dutch colonies further east, where these *Ikat* fabrics were believed to possess magical powers by the people of Indonesia and Malaya. The traders, in return, acquired Indonesia's spices, much in demand in Europe.

Thought to have originated in India around 700 AD, *Ikat* derives its name from the Malay word *Meningkat* which means to tie or bind. Unlike tie-dyed textiles, however, where an entire sheet is selectively knotted and tied and then dipped in various dyes, *Ikat* is distinguished by the fact that the warp and weft threads are tie-dyed separately before the cloth is woven. The distinctive fuzzy-edged patterns that distinguish *Ikat* textiles only begin to emerge when the individually dyed warp and weft threads are woven together. The skill behind this weaving and dying process lies in the ability to work out beforehand where these dyed sections will intersect and what pattern they will create, rather like a navigator plotting longitude and latitude to determine his position on a map. A complex and extremely time-consuming process, two weavers can often work together (on a loom that is specially tilted towards them so they can always see the patterns emerging) for more than a month to complete a single *sari*.

A designer who has combined this ancient Indian technique with contemporary design is Delhi-based designer Rakesh Thakore. Working simultaneously within the disciplines of fashion and interior design, his distinctive black-and-white *Ikat* textile designs (see pages 100, 101, 102, 164 and 165) are the result of his co-operation with the *Ikat* weavers of Orissa and Andhra Pradesh. Stimulated by the technical and marketing skills provided by the Government Hand-Loom Services Centres, these weavers have, for over 40 years, dominated the national hand-loom weaving market with beautifully made scarves, *saris* and furnishing fabrics.

One of the traditions of the *Ikat* weavers of Orissa and Andhra Pradesh has been the use of *Ikat* patterning to decorate the ends and borders of otherwise plain *dupattas* (shawls). Rakesh Thakore has taken this tradition and applied it to a range of elegant shawls which, with his sophisticated blend of Indian design and intuitive awareness of the Western fashion and design markets, have achieved critical and commercial success with the more exclusive retailers around the world.

Dhurries and Silks

Shyam Ahuja

India never developed a tradition of fine furniture. The floor was the surface on which all social interaction took place and rugs, therefore, play an important role in India's cultural history.

The use of rugs began in earnest in India with the arrival of the Muslims. Apart from their religious significance as prayer mats, carpets were considered to be essential possessions, no doubt because of the semi-nomadic lifestyle of their forefathers. Carpets were furniture, wealth and art all rolled into one. Even when they exchanged tents for palaces the importance of rugs remained. Delhi, Lahore and Agra became great centres of patronage for the creation of carpets and rugs. The preference was for knotted rugs with a raised pile, the form of expression that closely resembled and in many cases directly copied Persian traditions.

Following the decline of the Mughals, the Kachakawa rulers of Jaipur and Amber continued the tradition and commissioned enormous hand-knotted carpets from their own workshops. The flat, woven cotton rugs known as *dhurries*, also produced in workshops in Amber and Jaipur at that time, were used predominantly as underlays to protect the more valuable knotted rugs on top. Inspired by the Turkish and Persian flat weaves known as *kilims*, these inexpensive floor textiles were used extensively in Indian homes over the centuries, in many shapes, sizes and configurations. However, it was not until the late eighteenth century that *dhurries* started being used on their own by the Rajasthani ruling family to decorate the vast chambers and halls of the palaces. Often extending to over 25 metres in length and 10 metres in width, these royal commissions enhanced the development of rug-weaving and ensured the survival of this craft tradition to the present day.

Bombay-based designer and entrepeneur Shyam Ahuja can be considered the modern-day equivalent of these Maharajas. Developing, nurturing, supporting and challenging some 18,000 rug-weavers spread throughout villages in north-west India, he has established a company with an international reputation. His rugs, now sold in 30 countries, proved to be a light, versatile and unique alternative to traditional Persian carpets.

As Ahuja's international operation expands, so too does the range of products and the craft disciplines that are used to make them. Embroidery, leatherwork and block-printing are some of the village skills that he has started to utilize in an effort to seduce the Western consumer. In particular, Ahuja has had significant success with the introduction to Western markets of hand-loomed Indian silks. Raw silk is distinguished by the imperfect slubs in its weave which, when combined with typically bold and bright Indian colours, results in a textile of considerable aesthetic impact. As with *dhurries*, raw silks have become yet another example of an indigenous Indian handicraft that is enjoying a renaissance.

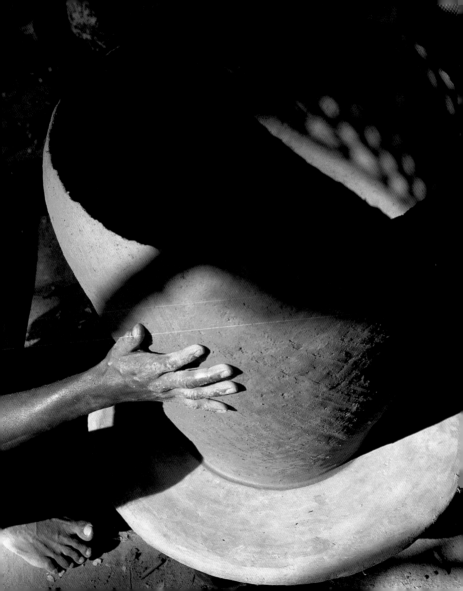

Terracotta

Ray Meeker

Nearly every village in India still has its own potter and it is estimated that there are over a million practitioners of the craft. Indeed, the potter has always been so thoroughly integrated into the rhythm of Indian life that even the Vedic scriptures did not classify him in a caste system which included other craftsmen; an indication of the importance of the role of this craft. This was further reinforced by the potter being accorded the mythical title of Prajapati or 'Lord of the People', which is believed to have been granted by Brahma himself as a reflection of his own creation of man by breathing life into a clay form.

Despite these divine associations, today the position of the village potter is in jeopardy. Plastic and aluminium have taken hold as cheap and convenient alternatives, even though they lack the natural insulating properties of terracotta. The tradition of displaying terracotta deities is also in decline. Religion is still a strong force in village life but gaily painted plaster and gilt pieces are now the preferred aesthetic. In an effort to embrace rather than reject these new influences, INTACH (the Indian National Trust for Arts and Cultural Heritage) has looked at ways of updating the skills of the potter in areas of design, technology and marketing. One such project is on a farm just south of Madras. Begun in 1992, groups of village potters from different regions of India are guided towards the production of larger, more elaborate decorative vessels and away from the production of predominantly utilitarian and inexpensive bowls, plates and jugs, in the hope that this will raise both the value and the quality of Indian terracotta ware. The notion of design as a value-added ingredient is also being taught, together with the introduction of the idea of producing for export markets.

Funded jointly by the Government and the Ford Foundation, the project is managed by Hans Kavshik, a sculptor, and Ray Meeker, an American architect/potter who has lived in India for the past 20 years. In an effort to leave less to chance and to promote a consistency in quality of colour and durability, particularly for the more elaborate pieces, the potters are being educated in the scientific principles of the different clays and glazes. Sources of clay are analysed for plasticity, natural colour and moisture content in a search for the ideal compound that will be easy to handle and that will not crack when dried in the sun or baked in a kiln.

Quite intentionally, the atmosphere at the farm, where the potters live for the duration of the course, parallels life on a university campus: the participants work and eat together and cultivate a professional camaraderie that contributes to an increased sense of pride in what they have learned and, more importantly, in what they already know. It is hoped that these potters will go back to their respective villages and spread their newly-learned techniques and knowledge to other craftsmen.

Block Printing

Faith Singh

In biblical times, the brightly coloured and sheer muslins of the Ganges Delta were India's most prized textiles; merchandise considered so precious by ancient civilizations that it was often included in the ransom demands of victorious conquerors as the price they would exact for showing mercy. With the discovery of India by the European nations the *chhapai* (block-printed cloth), decorated with exotic patterns imitating foliage and flowers in colours that were like 'painted sunlight', transformed European fashion and interior decoration.

Ironically, the success of Indian *chhapai* in Europe had catastrophic consequences in India. The initial success of the fabrics led to rapid production, but then the Europeans began to produce their own cheap machine-printed cloth and demand slumped, throwing thousands of Indians out of work.

Today, however, hand block-printed textiles are once again enjoying export success. In a world bored with machine-made regularity, the character of these handmade fabrics offers a small, colourful respite from manufactured fabrics. Revitalized by the All India Handicrafts Board in the 1950s with the development of training schools, the production of block-printed cotton remains a living skill. The technique of hand-block printing is relatively simple: a timber block with a carved face on one side is dipped in dye and pressed directly onto the fabric. Skill is required to ensure that subsequent stamps are of equal colour and appear as one continuous pattern.

The northwestern states of Rajasthan and Gujarat are still the main production areas, as they have been for more than 400 years. Jaipur and Amber, in particular, recognized as the leading centres of cloth-printing skills due partially to the marketing success of Jaipur's enterprizing traders. Unfortunately, however, in order to meet this growing demand from international markets, many artisans are beginning to print cloth in partly mechanized workshops and are using the cheaper more easily available chemical dyes; a practice that could prove to be very destructive because it is putting the original appeal of the block-printed cloth in jeopardy.

Only a small number of firms continue to work in the slow and expensive traditional methods. One such firm is Anokhi, a company that has attempted to preserve traditional techniques and methods, such as using vegetable-based dyes, by introducing design into the equation. Firmly committed to Rajasthan's creative heritage, John and Faith Singh are convinced that success can only be achieved if the 'product' is kept in step with the demands of the modern world. Employing a team of freelance designers as well as contributing a series of designs herself, Faith Singh has taken what was an attractive but rather staid craft into the realm of a design business which welcomes fresh ideas, colours, patterns and designs.

178

PAGE 152
Terracotta pots sit against an outside wall of designer Asha Sarabhai's studio in Ahmedabad. Gujarat. Appreciation of the skills of India's village artisans has been actively promoted by India's community of contemporary designers. who have played a critical role in re-establishing and re-defining the relevance of village craft traditions.

PAGE 154
The production of textiles in India is an ancient tradition. Asha Sarabhai is a textile designer who. as a modern proponent of this tradition. is concerned with the expression of an aesthetic in fabrics that is at once indigenous yet contemporary. By mixing traditional techniques with new ideas. she has produced a range of fabrics that in their unbleached state highlight the inherent texture of the cloth.

PAGES 156-157
Asha Sarabhai's sense of design focuses on new ways of looking at the familiar. by drawing on existing techniques and extending them into a contemporary context. Her latest range of fabrics are refined. subtle and minimal. and cleverly obscure the labour-intensive complexity of the detailing. On her cushion covers created in *Kora*. the Indian term for loom-state. the minute ornamentation consists of tiny pieces of coloured silk woven into the folds of the fabric.

PAGES 158
Blue pottery was brought to Jaipur in the sixteenth century by Muslim invaders who had discovered it in Persia. The early craftsmen went to great lengths to keep the process a secret and they were so successful that it quickly died out. Kripal Singh set out to revive the process and it took many years of hard work and research to piece together the clues that history had left behind. Today. Jaipur blue pottery is once again thriving and is widely available.

PAGES 160-161
Jaipur blue pottery is unusual not just because of its colour but also because of its composition. The pottery contains no clay and is instead a mixture of quartz. glass. gum. fuller's earth and sodium carbonate. The distinctive colours and decoration are created from the browns and blacks of copper and cobalt oxide. which only become bright blue once the pottery has been fired.

PAGE 162
Like Asha Sarabhai. Rakesh Thakore is concerned with the reinterpretation of traditional skills. Experimenting with the *Ikat* method of weaving. which originated in India. he has developed an elegant and refined range of minimal geometric scarves.

PAGES 164-165
Hanging in the courtyard of a traditional Rajasthani stone house, these scarves designed by Rakesh Thakore attest to the potential of design originating from India. Sold in the most exclusive department stores in Japan, these sophisticated pieces of weaving support Thakore's argument that items made by hand ought, especially in an increasingly automated world, to be valued more highly than products that are machine-made.

PAGE 166
Working with a network of approximately 18,000 weavers spread throughout the villages of India, Shyam Ahuja has become one of the world's largest and most successful suppliers of rugs to the interior design industry. Utilizing the skills of the village weavers, Ahuja has built a reputation for quality by importing the finest of raw ingredients for these craftsmen to work with: wool from New Zealand, silk from China, linen from Ireland and cotton from Egypt.

PAGES 168-169
Shyam Ahuja has also ventured into textiles. One of his successful design contributions has been the marketing of Indian raw silk in the West. Different from the silks one is accustomed to from China or Thailand, raw silk is distinguished by its imperfections – the raised slubs that give the fabric more body and character – and its brighter and bolder colour.

PAGE 170 The tradition of terracotta is as old as India itself. The challenge today is to translate this ancient medium into a material relevant in the twentieth century. A project funded by the Central Government and the Ford Foundation aims to infuse traditional terracotta pot-making with modern techniques and to train India's village potters to become more aware of design and marketing.

PAGES 172-173
The value of handicraft, particularly if it is culturally authentic, is increasingly being recognized and India's 3,000-year-old tradition of terracotta pot-making is in a strong position to benefit from this growing appreciation. Village potters, who once would have been kept busy making waterjugs for the villagers, can now afford to concentrate their efforts on the more challenging and intricate task of making larger pieces, such as those in this photograph.

PAGE 174
Anokhi, a company set up by John and Faith Singh to preserve, adapt and market traditional hand-block printing techniques, employs Rajasthani villagers to produce textile designs that are indigenous, original and commercial. The village craftsmen do their own hand-dyeing in boiling vats of water over an open fire, while the hand-block printing process takes place inside local *havelis* and homes. These yarns, having just come out of the dye vat, are left in the sandy soil to dry.

PAGES 176-177
The process of printing on cloth with wooden blocks is relatively simple and takes place throughout Rajasthan: the block is dipped in dye and then pressed directly onto the fabric. Yet it took the design input of Faith Singh to redefine this village tradition and create a modern and marketable product. The resulting fabrics, such as these indigo bed covers, are now sold all over the world.

6
Ornate Order

A mania for organizing life can be found
in the countless distinctions of language,
caste, religious sects and gods. Even the
most famous erotic sculptures are, at one
level, an almost out-of-control attempt
to list and categorize every conceivable
sexual position as a metaphor for the
wild abundance of humanity.

Steven R. Weisman

Ornate Order

Babur, descendant of Timur and Genghis Khan, conqueror of India and first ruler of the Mughal dynasty, was an avid horticulturalist and lover of architecture. A keen and accurate observer, he left behind a magnificent 40-page account of his first impressions of the newly conquered Hindustan (India), in which he marvels at the existing social structure, the caste system, the Indian method of counting and keeping time, the profusion of erotic sculptures in stone and the extraordinary abundance of India's craftsmen. His writing revealed a particular fascination with the Indian mania for organizing life and obsession with order.

Polka-dotted cow's horns, elaborately decorated buildings, bejewelled villagers, roadside shrines festooned with garlands of coloured tinsel – the decorative flair that extends to almost every aspect of life in India is legendary. Yet what may appear to the visitor as a carnival of decorative indulgence, an apparently frivolous frenzy of adornment, goes a lot deeper than mere beautification: it is part of a system of order with profound meaning and purpose that reflects a pervasive and intense spirituality.

This notion of ornate order, a decorative approach to structure within society, is present in every facet of life in India, even the bedroom. Far from being a manual for promoting sexual promiscuity, as it is usually perceived, the *Karma Sutra* is an evocatively illustrated guide to every sexual position which was conceived by the Brahmin priests as a practical answer to India's vulnerability to invasion. The priests believed in the concept of 'safety in numbers', and consciously set out to create a guide for procreation.

The expression of ornate order has its most powerful legacy in India's architectural heritage. Out of complex spiritual origins India's architects developed a predilection for the abstract and so laid the foundation for combining complexity and simplicity to great visual effect. A fine example of this skill is shown in the *jali* colonnade of Akbar's tomb (see pages 196 and 197). The corridor lined with carved stone *jali*, the traditional Islamic window treatment, initially appears to be a classic example of typical Moorish architecture with a strict repetition of geometric forms. But closer inspection reveals that the pattern of each *jali* is entirely different and that, whereas the eye might be tricked into seeing repetition, they are, indeed, arranged at random. Order, however, is still achieved by subjugating the randomly patterned *jali* to the repetition of the arches in which they are framed.

This asymmetry within symmetry proved to be an effective visual tool for the architects of the Mughal period and, as was the case with the finer aspects of the Mughal courts, it was later imitated by the Kachakawa rulers of Rajasthan. Hundreds of years later this unique visual device also proved to be a source of major inspiration for two of the world's most renowned modernists: Louis Kahn and Le Corbusier.

We have always been a decorative people.

Ram Rahman

The Palace Tent of Shah Jahan

Shah Jahan, son of Jahangir, grandson of the great Emperor Akbar, was one of the world's greatest patrons of the arts. His crowning glory, for which he will always be remembered, is the Taj Mahal, the apotheosis of all Islamic architecture. Yet, despite Shah Jahan's reputation as a great patron of architectural extravagances, little is known about his mobile structures.

Shah Jahan's ancestors lived a semi-nomadic existence near Kabul and setting up tents became one of the most important rituals, giving order and stability to their nomadic lifestyle. Later, when the Mughals conquered northern India and established themselves near Delhi, this semi-nomadic heritage influenced the design of their more permanent structures. Some of their tents had been unimaginably elaborate in their design and construction, and this was reflected in the building of the capital city of the Mughal Empire, Fatehpur Sikri, by Akbar. Constructed in stone and marble, the free-standing pavilions recall the semi-nomadic lifestyle of his ancestors.

Shah Jahan was a prolific builder of temples and palaces, and his palace workshop was renowned for having the very best craftsmen, architects, engineers and artists that could be found. Thus, inspired by the majesty of his own creations in marble and stone, he commissioned his workshop to make a tent the like of which the world had never seen. More a portable palace than a tent, Shah Jahan wanted a mobile structure that would recreate the intricacies and formalities of life at court while he was away from his established seat of government waging war or hunting.

Believed to have been confiscated as a result of a lost battle with a Rajput ruler from Jodphur, who would have had little practical use for such an extravagance, this splendid tent was relegated to a forgotten corner of Jodphur's Meherangarh Fort for over 300 years. It has survived almost completely intact because for most of that time it has not been exposed to the damaging effects of sunlight.

Anthropology has taught us that the world
is differently defined in different places. It
is not only that people have different gods
and expect different post-mortem fates. It
is, rather, that the worlds of different
peoples have different shapes.

Walter Goldschmidt

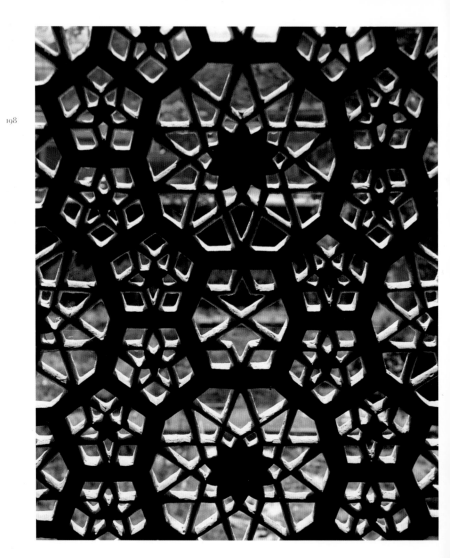

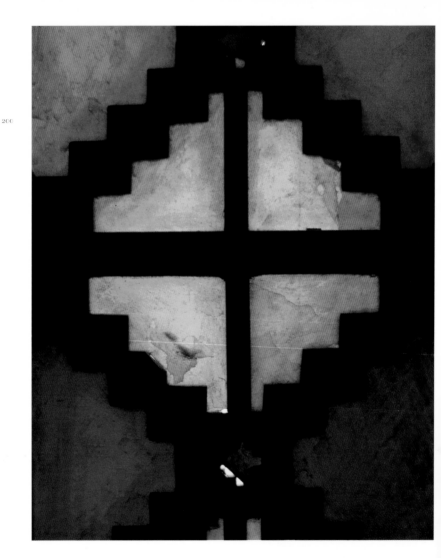

200

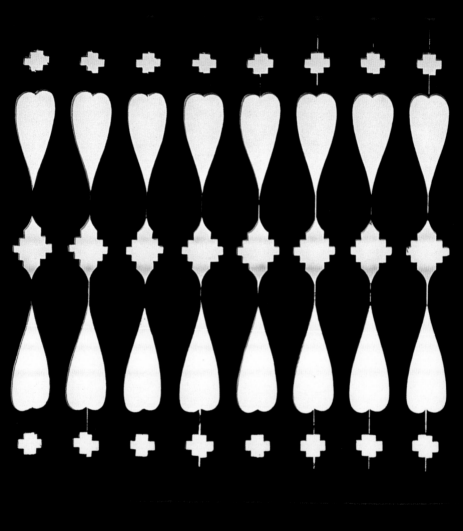

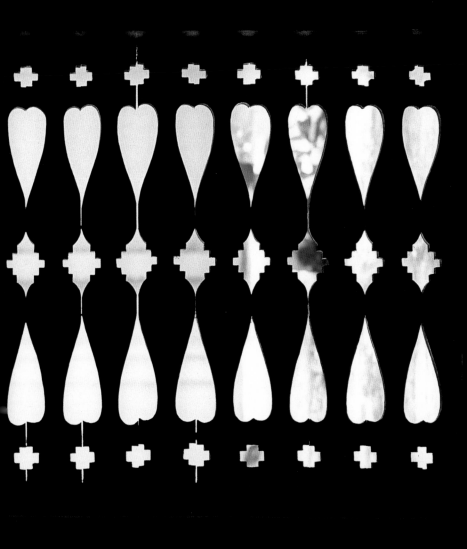

PAGES 182

The decorative detailing of this archway in the Jaipur City Palace, built by Maharaja Jai Singh II in *c*.1728, is a testament to the extra-ordinary levels of skill that were attained by the craftsmen of the time. Virtually every artisan discipline is represented in the palace. This single piece of work practically explodes with detail, yet an instinctive design sense stops this complex piece of embellishment from being ostentatious – no simple task, given the number of colours, textures and shapes used.

PAGES 184-185

A cluster of carved hands at the gate of Meherangarh Fort, Jodhpur; each one a symbol of *sati*. *Sati*, meaning literally 'honourable woman', is the voluntary act of a wife taking her own life following her husband's death, usually by immolation on his funeral pyre. Upon leaving their home to go to the funeral pyre each *sati* would place her hand-print on the wall; this imprint would then be carved out of the stone and anointed with red dye and silver lead. The practice of *sati* was outlawed by the British in the early nineteenth century, but there are a number of places in India where it still occurs.

PAGE 186

A 24-carat gold pendant and medallion, photographed on a man at the annual Pushkar Camel Fair, illustrates the natural affinity for decoration that extends to every aspect of life.

PAGES 188-189

The silver jewellery worn by the tribal and nomadic women of north India reveals, in its brilliant, showy, glittering excess, a deep love of adornment. Yet there is a practical side to this elaborate decorative display. In a nation historically subject to invasion and conquest, the notion of 'portable wealth' is appropriate; women literally 'wear what they are worth'.

PAGES 190-191

Like permanent parasols dotted around the countryside, *chhatri* are small mausoleums that were built to commemorate and protect the dead. Distinguished by their hexagonal or octagonal plans, and by the ornate columns that support the dome that sits on top, a group of *chhatri* just outside Jodhpur, with their profusion of elaborately carved columns, highlights the uniquely Indian concept of ornate order.

PAGE 192

Discovered by accident in the dungeons of Meherangarh Fort, Jodhpur, this portable cloth palace is constructed from the most sumptuous and robust red silk velvet, embroidered with gold and silver metal-wrapped yarns. Used as Shah Jahan's home and seat of government when he was away on hunting expeditions or waging war and complete with fabric archways and elaborate inner sanctums, it sought to create a portable version of the intricate aspects of life at court.

PAGE 194

Carved out of a single slab of stone, *jali* were first introduced to India by the Mughals and are now firmly part of Indian architectural tradition. The hand-carved, mesh screen filters light and maintains privacy and security while allowing air to enter and circulate inside. Because of the high temperatures in India, glazed windows are undesirable and impractical and, as a result, traditional *jali* are now being incorporated into modern Indian architecture.

PAGES 196-197

A *jali* colonnade at Akbar's tomb, Sikandra, built in memory of Emperor Akbar (1542-1605), provides a dazzling decorative display when a burst of sunlight is projected through the screens of this marble gallery. The seemingly random combination of *jali* patterns is constrained by the mathematical discipline of the repeated form of identical arches. The tension caused by the combination of chaos and restraint is a hallmark of Indian creativity.

PAGE 198

The geometric decoration of *jali* is a reflection of its Islamic origins. The Koran forbids the representation of people or animals, hence the design of the Mughal stone fretwork screens was limited to abstract geometrics.

PAGE 199

The royal family of Udaipur have traditionally used the sun as the symbol of their lineage and, as a consequence, there is no shortage of images of the sun in and around the Maharanas' palaces in Udaipur. Perhaps the most interesting of them is this brass impression in the City Palace. The plaque, the size of a person's face, is actually a hinged porthole. On ceremonial occasions in the past, and to the absolute delight of the crowds waiting below, the Maharana would open the plaque from the inside and reveal his face through the circular void.

PAGE 200

Unlike the north of India, where most building is in stone or mud, the traditional houses and palaces of the south are often built entirely of timber, in a style that, although Hindu in origin, is more Far Eastern in appearance. This vividly coloured window, made out of mica, is a detail from the council chamber of the sixteenth-century Padmanabhapuram Palace in Kerala.

PAGE 201

In the remote desert town of Jaisalmer, near the border of Pakistan, windows are usually screened with traditional *jali* carved in stone. Occasionally, however, one is replaced by a pierced metal *jali*. In this *haveli* window, the popular Hindu peacock motif has been superbly integrated; evidence of the rich and illustrious Indian tradition of decorative metalwork. As the maker of weapons, the metalworker in antiquity was accorded a high status. From these practical beginnings, metalworkers still produce an extraordinarily diverse range of ornate goods, from elaborate decorative locks to brass water pots, fine bronze icons and statues of popular deities.

PAGES 202-203

Padmanabhapuram Palace in Kerala is one of the oldest and best preserved wooden buildings in India. A beautiful pagoda-shaped monument, it is distinguished by the quality of its joinery and by the fine decorative detailing of its woodwork. These timber *jali* panels, inside the main banquet hall of the centrally placed Thai Kottaram (Mother Palace), decorate the circumference of the hall and at the same time fulfil the task of keeping heat and light out while allowing air to circulate. A classic example of the notion of ornate order.

7

Form Follows Culture

Architecture is a cultural instrument.

Louis I. Kahn

Form Follows Culture

Indian architecture is beginning to find its own way; for the contemporary Indian architect the central challenge lies in striking a balance between *change* – the driving force for any culture – and *continuity*, the link with the past which provides architecture with a cultural resonance. Current architecture in India presents a vast and confusing proliferation of styles, scales and ideologies, and this is being further added to by architects who merely imitate the latest trends from the industrial world. However, while there does not appear to be a common visual approach to the new architecture being built in India today, it is possible to discern an emerging commonality of approach: not a style as we would know it but more a matter of shared inspiration.

This rather vague (by Western standards) movement is highly appropriate in a culture that has historically been uninterested in rigid definition. Whereas Western values such as technology and reason have forced a certain 'rationalization' of form and expression, the values prevalent in India, of spiritualism, tradition and the cyclical nature of life, have predisposed the nation's architects towards a more abstract approach to their work. Consequently, modern architecture in India, although it might well make use of Western technology, does not share the ideological dogma of the industrialized world. There is no pressure on India's architects to conform to set standards of style. Buildings do not have to look alike to be alike.

Drawing on India's spiritualism, architectural design is beginning to utilize what Romi Khosla describes as 'invented authenticity', a strong if not immediately obvious link connecting with the soul, not the eyes. A distinctly Indian approach, it relies on the *spirit* of the building to evoke a sense of continuity or belonging. This notion of 'invented authenticity' is not so concerned with appearances as it is with sources of inspiration. If these are appropriate and authentic, then the building, in whatever form it takes and in whatever material, will be Indian in the truest, spiritual sense. This is an architecture that reflects a shared state of mind as opposed to a shared visual style.

Two contemporary architectural projects, Satish Gujral's Belgian Embassy in Delhi and Charles Correa's Jawahar Kala Kendra Museum in Jaipur, present the most powerful and vivid examples of this emerging Indian approach of shared inspiration. Entirely different in form, shape, colour and material, these two commissions appear to have nothing in common, but as their source or basis of their design they share the same 'entry point': the *mandala*, an influential factor in Indian architecture since the start of Hindu civilization. Since the *mandala* can take an extraordinary number of different forms, the constructions bear no resemblance to each other, but they succeed in sharing a commonality of approach and are as a result unmistakably Indian.

The Belgian Embassy

Satish Gujral

In 1980, the world-renowned Indian artist, Satish Gujral, was commissioned to design the Belgian Embassy and the Ambassador's residence in New Delhi's embassy row, a veritable showcase of modern architecture. Satish Gujral had already made a name for himself in India 30 years earlier with his powerfully graphic, figurative paintings reflecting the agony which the new nation was having to endure as a result of partition. Following great acclaim, Gujral's work took him to Mexico where he worked with Siqueros and other modern masters and developed a strong interest in the mural as a public art form. Charged by his Mexican experience, Gujral returned to India and became a major muralist, creating huge ceramic murals on public buildings in Delhi. Through his work with murals he became increasingly involved with architecture and acutely aware of the relationship between the two; an awareness that eventually led him to abandon murals in favour of a more comprehensive expression. He turned instead to sculpture and, in his own distinctive response to the Tantric art movement that was raging at the time (late 1960s-early 1970s), began to create abstract three-dimensional expressions in wood and metal that, in a sense, translated the symmetrical *Yantra* drawings, such as the *mandala*, from flat grids to complex planar and spheroid forms. His graphic, symmetrical handling of volume resulted in three-dimensional interpretations of these ancient Hindu configurations. Sculpturally, Gujral had tapped into the deepest wells of Indian spirituality and it is these influences that he brought with him to architecture.

Thus, the designer of the Belgian Embassy was neither architect nor engineer. He was a famous Indian artist, who was presented with an opportunity to express his work on an unprecedented scale. Indeed, the fact that he was not an architect actually proved to be a distinct advantage, as Indian architectural photographer and journalist Ram Rahman explains: 'Without the baggage of an academically trained modernist, Gujral has not had to agonize over trying to create a synthesis between the "Indian" and the modern, a problem being fought out for two decades now in the Indian architectural scene. As he has said numerous times, "I just want to design" and came up with possibly the most Indian building in the last twenty years.'

As a result, it is difficult to define Gujral's direct influences but the indirect influences are clear. The Belgian Ambassador's residence emerged from Gujral's *mandala*-inspired sculpture, almost as if his three-dimensional interpretations of this ancient Hindu configuration had been magically enlarged into a building, creating in the process a piece of architecture that is Indian in the most profound way.

The ruins of numerous empires are
evoked by these walls, and rhyme
with other monuments scattered
throughout this old city.

Ram Rahman

Jawahar Kala Kendra Museum

Charles Correa

Not unlike Jai Singh II, whose innovative ideas and progressive thinking led to the creation of Jaipur as the first planned city in the world, architect Charles Correa combines the curiosity of a scientist and the introspection of an intellectual with the determination of a leader. His primary concern lies in creating a future without ignoring or destroying the past. As he says, 'Each generation has to reinvent its culture in a new material. It's a question of transformation, not just a transfer of images from the past.' For Correa architecture should be invention within a defined mandate and scope; inventing anything that comes to mind is seen by him as a foolish indulgence and he sees no challenge in it.

Correa's approach is clear in the commission to design the Jawahar Kala Kendra Museum in Jaipur. For the design he combined all the forces that have been significant in his own architecture to date with the most salient and emotive aspects of Jaipur's history, especially the motivation behind the initial design and planning of the city by Jai Singh. Correa has made a lifelong study of defining Indian architecture and here he has created a thoroughly modern building that reverberates with all the powerful resonance of India's rich, exotic culture.

Central to Correa's design are the sun and the number nine. Correa sees the sun as the dominant force in daily life in India and as such it is also the determining factor in this project. In creating an elaborate series of transitions from outdoor to indoor spaces, Correa has provided a metaphor for the sun while recalling a design feature of Hindu and Jain places of worship: the notion of interchangeable open and enclosed space has been a feature of the monumental temples and shrines of India since antiquity. The movement between the pavilions, or *mahals*, which make up the form of the museum is also important in presenting a more dynamic setting in which to display work by craftsmen and artists. Mimicking the streets, markets and alleyways of India in which their work would normally be displayed, the spaces between the *mahals* present a natural and more emotive area for displaying craft, adding another powerful metaphor to the design of the building and doing away with the frequently alienating stuffiness of most museums.

As a basic plan for Jawahar Kala Kendra Museum, Charles Correa invoked the nine-square *mandala*, a Tantric equation that in ancient Hindu mythology represented a model of the universe and which since the beginning of civilization in India has been used as the mathematical basis for architecture. The *mandala* Correa referred to for his museum is believed to be the same as that used by Jai Singh 300 years earlier for the plan of his new city. The number nine is the most spiritual of all numbers and has a powerful presence in Hindu mythology: it is supposed to connect man to the universe and it is related mathematically to both Hindu cosmology and astrology.

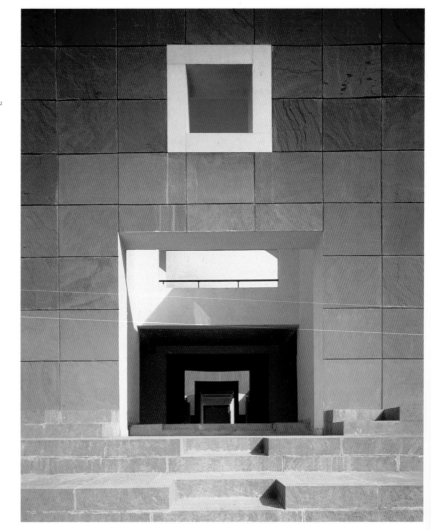

PAGE 208
The design of the Belgian Ambassador's residence in Delhi suggests the direction contemporary Indian architecture may take in the future. The notion of endowing a modern building with a distinct regional identity has shown the potential for India to reclaim its cultural identity through its architecture. In this case Satish Gujral's design, with its exterior textures of local granite and brick, rhythmically constructed with diagonal lines and sweeping brick arches, evokes the ruins of numerous empires spread throughout Delhi, in particular those which have given Delhi its nickname: 'City of Tombs'.

PAGE 210
The interior of the residence plays on vertical, horizontal and diagonal geometrics. The foyer, rising more than two storeys in height, is distinguished by an intricately conceived series of skylights set into a cross-vaulted dome which can be seen from the outside (see page 208).

PAGES 212-213
Virtually invisible from the street, the Belgian Ambassador's residence is set into a vast sunken garden. It is at once a reminder of the pleasures of the Persian sunken garden, and a clever and effective solution to the need for privacy and security.

PAGES 214-215
In contrast to the earthy materials of the exterior, the interior of white-painted brick and ceramic tiles creates a cool impression. A cascade of white marble stairs leads left and right from the entrance lobby, repeating and reinforcing the rhythmic lines and shapes that run through the entire building. The main living and entertaining area of the Belgian Ambassador's residence is essentially a diamond shape, part of the overall *mandala*-inspired design. The converging diagonals of this diamond shape are a fireplace at one end, and the entrance lobby at the other.

PAGE 216
Gujral used local materials such as Delhi granite and baked brick in the construction of the building, but its forms are drawn entirely from his sculpture. Inspired by Tantric *mandalas*, he literally carved the forms out of the ground. It is as if his imagination has recreated the architectural remnants of India's past.

PAGE 218
The Jawahar Kala Kendra Museum of arts and crafts in Jaipur, designed by Charles Correa, is dedicated to the first Prime Minister of independant India, Jawaharlal Nehru. The building is a synthesis of the most important aspects of physical and spiritual Indian culture. No opportunity has been wasted to make the building relate to the people; even less significant details, such as the typical Rajasthani timber door and the small, square windows that are also found in ancient forts, reinforce the effort made by Correa to create a building that is at once proudly and recognizably Indian, and indisputably modern.

PAGES 220-221
Rajasthan is famous for its red sandstone which was used to build the temples, palaces and forts of the Mughal rulers, and later by Sir Edwin Lutyens in his designs for New Delhi. Correa chose to make use of this distinctive Rajasthani material for the outside walls that enclose the concrete-frame museum. Each wall is a massive 90 metres long and is topped with a beige Dholpur capping-stone that runs its entire length. The planetary symbols of each *mahal* (house) are represented on the outside walls in inlaid white marble, embellished with black granite and mica slate.

PAGE 222
The monumental passageway into the museum reveals the layering of the *mahals*, and creates a seemingly effortless and natural interchange between interior and exterior space that reinforces the elemental nature of Correa's design: a reverence for the dominating aspect of daily life in India – the sun. The extensive use of cut-outs, windows and stairways provides a reference to human scale in enormous spaces that would otherwise be overpowering. The object of the design is to involve, not to intimidate.

PAGE 223
A view from the Guru Mahal into the Surya Mahal, an open-air plaza or *kund* that offers a resting place for visitors, and a performance space for traditional Rajasthani music, dance and theatre. The Surya Mahal is the centre square in the nine-square plan of the museum. The circle at its centre is a symbol of the sun.

PAGES 224-225
The success of this museum lies not only in the spiritually and historically appropriate way it has been designed, but also in the way the *mahals* relate to each other. With the clever use of open spaces, visitors are invited to wander along the streets and alleyways of these micro-cities which create a living setting for craftspeople to present their work.

PAGE 226
The Jawahar Kala Kendra Museum is probably the finest example to date of the application of Indian myth and legend in a contemporary building form. As such, it is an important contribution to the on-going struggle to define 'an architecture of the nation'. Based on the *navagraha mandala*, a Tantric energy-field represented by a grid of nine squares (concept on which the city of Jaipur was originally planned), Correa has created the museum out of nine square houses or *mahals*. The intricately designed *mahals*, each constructed in a different colour, represent the individual purposes of the structures. The domed ceiling inside the Manghal Mahal symbolizes arrival, and the mural, one of several by contemporary Indian artists in the museum, was included in the design to show that wall-painting in India is a living art.

PAGE 227
The domed ceiling of the Manghal Mahal is painted with a mural representing a Jain cosmograph (see pages 20 and 21). The cosmograph is a depiction of part of the middle world (Jain cosmology is divided into three worlds: upper, middle and lower) from which the soul can gain release. In a clever use of the symbolism, the absolute centre of the cosmograph, which normally constitutes an illustration, is a hole in the dome through which one can view the sky.

I like the evening in India, the one magic
moment when the sun balances on the
rim of the world, and the hush descends,
and ten thousand civil servants drift
homeward on a river of bicycles, brooding
on the Lord Krishna and the cost of living.

James Cameron

Bibliography

236

Nicholas Barnard, *The Arts and Crafts of India*, Conran Octopus, London, 1993

Stafford Cliff and Suzanne Slesin, *Indian Style*, Thames & Hudson, London, 1990

Roger Connah, 'Satish Gujral' in *Inside Outside*, February-March 1987

Bamber Gascoigne, *The Great Moghuls*, Jonathan Cape, London, 1971

Carmen Kagal (ed.), *Vistara – The Architecture of India*, exhibition catalogue, Bombay, 1986

Madhu Jain, 'Charles Correa – Building the Future with the Spirit of the Past' in *India Today* (Bombay), 15 May 1992

Romi Khosla, 'Current Architecture in India' in *Mimar* (Singapore), 41, 1992

Romi Khosla, 'The Profoundness of the Middle View of Architecture', unpublished conference paper, New Delhi, January 1992

Neelam Mathews, *Classic Indian Handicrafts*, Rupa & Co., New Delhi, 1993

Aman Nath, *Jaipur – The Last Destination*, India Book House, Bombay, 1993

Aman Nath and Francis Wacziarg, *The Arts and Crafts of Rajasthan*, Mapin, New Delhi, 1985

Ram Rahman, 'Satish Gujral – Four Decades' in *Architecture & Design* (New Delhi), July-August 1987

Christopher Tadgell, *The History of Architecture in India*, Phaidon Press, London, 1993

Uma Vasuder, 'Satish Gujral – Where the Intensities Burn' in *India Perspectives* (New Delhi), 39, July 1991

Francis Watson, *India – A Concise History*, Thames & Hudson, London, 1979

Stanley Wolpert, *A New History of India*, 4th edition, Oxford University Press, 1993

Paul Zaveri and Nimish Patel, 'Heritage Fabric and Conservation Movement: Keys to the Conservation of Living Settlements', notes for presentation at the International Conference on Architectural Heritage, Bombay, January 1992

Acknowledgements

SYDNEY Special thanks goes to Vinod Kumar and G.S. Sachdev of the Government of India Tourist Office for the marvellous job they did in organizing our tour. Without their research, advice and sponsorship the project would never have taken place.

Special thanks also go to Melanie De Souza (Oberoi Hotels International) and Judy Chapman (TCI Travel Corporation India Ltd).

NEW DELHI It was my extreme good fortune that Ram Rahman was on hand in Delhi when we were there. Ram made all the right introductions for us and through his network of connections we were lucky enough to stumble across many more ideas and projects than we would otherwise have found.

Special thanks also go to Sanjiv Kr. Vashist, Narenda Kothiyal (Government of India Tourist Office); Regini Chopra, Anuradha Chopra, Indira Banerji (Oberoi Hotels International); Behram P. Dumasia, Arun Rastogi, Ajay Seth, Inderjeet Sohrawat (TCI Ltd); David Abraham, Hooshang Anvari, Romi Khosla, Bronwyn and Salim Latif, Aman Nath, Her Excellency, the Ambassadress, Mrs Funes-Noppon, Martand Singh, Rakesh Thakore and Francis Wacziarg.

JAIPUR I owe a great debt of gratitude to Faith and John Singh. Their own enthusiasm for India's indigenous culture is infectious and their commitment to projects such as the restoration of the historic *haveli* in Amber, the exemplary design of their own farmhouse on the outskirts of Jaipur, and their international textile business built on the strength of village tradition, provided both subject matter and inspiration.

Special thanks also go to S.R. Menna (Government of India Tourist Office); Tara Deva (TCI Ltd); Dharmendar Kanwar, Rajiv Khanna, Romanie Jaitly, Brigitte and Sunny Singh, and Kripal Singh.

AHMEDABAD Special thanks go to Nimish Patel for devoting so much of his time to show us around Ahmedabad and for providing us with an insight into the state of contemporary Indian architecture. His own active participation in the heritage preservation movement was a crucial contribution to the research for the section on renovation in this book.

Special thanks also go to Dr Fateh Singh (Commissioner of Tourism, Government of Gujarat); Hemant Pradhan (Tourism Corporation of Gujarat Ltd); Sudhir Dalal, Asha Sarabhai, and Parul Zaveri.

BOMBAY Without hesitation I can say that Charles Correa was the catalyst for this project. The first example of contemporary Indian architecture I ever saw was in a monograph dedicated to his work, published by *Mimar*. It was this that encouraged me to organize the tour that ultimately resulted in this book. Charles Correa, for me, is living proof that it is, indeed, possible to be thoroughly 'modern' and 'Indian' at the same time.

Special thanks go to C. Srinivas, Mrs T. Devichand, Jeanette da Silva, Meera Devidayal (Government of India Tourist Office); Mr Ratan Tata, Sarosh Aibara, Joanne Pereira, Firoze J. Darbary (Oberoi Hotels International); Shyam Ahuja, Uday B. Ajgaonkar, Preeti Bedi, Charles and Monika Correa, Sadrudin H. Daya, Roshan M. Kalaposi, Anuradha Mahindra, Rahul Mehrotra, Padmini G. Mirchandani, and Professor R.S. Vartack, Sir J.J. College of Architecture.

TRIVANDRUM Klaus Schleusener proved an inspiration and a great help in taking our appreciation for Indian culture one step further. In addition to being very knowledgeable on the subject of traditional architecture in Kerala, he also taught us to appreciate traditional Indian music by arranging an unforgettable concert, at sunset, on his magnificent promontory overlooking the southern Indian Ocean.

Special thanks also go to V. Balaram and Babu Varghose (Tourindia).

MADRAS Deborah Thiagarajan introduced me to the terracotta training project that she helped establish, as Madras director of INTACH, on a farm outside Madras. This project not only provided some beautiful photographic opportunities but also, more importantly, it showed that the relevance of 'craft' in the modern world is often only a matter of redefining the customer.

Special thanks also go to Nooruneesa Jam (Government of India Tourist Office); Shreyas Nair (Oberoi Hotels International); Bruce Robson, Bernard Rangaswami (TCI Ltd), and Ray Meeker.

LONDON I would like to thank the staff at Phaidon Press for their commitment to this book.

Special thanks also go to Brian Richards and Stafford Cliff.

Photography

It goes without saying that *India Modern* would never have progressed beyond the idea stage if it were not for the talents of the photographic team whose work powerfully captures the positive expressions and expectations of India's contemporary craftsmen. Each photographer brought a special talent to this project and it is the collective strength of their specializations from which *India Modern* ultimately benefits.

ROY LEWIS A graduate of the Royal College of Art, Roy Lewis emigrated to Australia in 1967 where he subsequently became head of the Design Department at Randwick TAFE, one of Sydney's leading art colleges. In 1988 Lewis decided to leave the education system and take up photography full-time. In a relatively short period of time he has established himself as a photographer with one of the best portfolios on India. His background in graphic design is evident in his superb portraits of village people and his powerful recordings of India's magnificent architectural legacies. His photos appear on pages 2 and 3, 4 and 5, 6 and 7, 16, 22 and 23, 24, 26 and 27, 28, 34, 36, 38, 40 and 41, 42, 45, 46 and 47, 48, 50 and 51, 75, 76 and 77, 78 and 79, 120, 122 and 123, 124 and 125, 126 and 127, 128 and 129, 130 and 131, 132 and 133, 134 and 135, 136 and 137, 138 and 139, 140 and 141, 142 and 143, 144, 146 and 147, 182, 184 and 185, 186, 188 and 189, 190 and 191, 192, 198, 201, 202 and 203, 230, 232 and 234.

WILLEM RETHMEIER Dutch-born Willem Rethmeier, a graduate of Holland's elite Rietveldt Art Academy, began to specialize in interior and architectural photography shortly after he first moved to Sydney in 1981. A widely published photographer of interior photography on the international scene, his photos are recognized by their painterly compositions. In India his contribution was invaluable in recording on film the style and ambience of some of the projects described in this book. His photos appear on pages 65, 67, 70 and 71, 73, 94 and 95, 98, 100 and 101, 103, 104 and 105, 110, 114 and 115, 154, 156 and 157, 158, 160 and 161, 166, 168 and 169, 174, 176 and 177, 194, 200, 210, 214 and 215.

TREVOR MEIN Originally trained as an architect, Trevor Mein discovered his talent for capturing form on film when he began to photograph collectors' cars for his brother's car magazine in which the cars appeared as magnificent pieces of mobile architecture. This rather obtuse introduction led to increasing amounts of work and eventual specialization in architectural photography. His background in architecture is obviously an enormous help in the direction he has chosen and on our travels it was Trevor who captured the glory of historic as well as modern Indian architecture. His photos appear on pages 18, 30, 32 and 33, 52, 58, 60 and 61, 62, 66, 68 and 69, 90, 106, 108 and 109, 112 and 113, 152, 162, 164 and 165, 170, 172 and 173.

RAM RAHMAN Indian-born, Rahman was educated in the USA at MIT, and went on to gain a master's degree in Fine Arts at Yale. He now divides his time between assignments in New Delhi and New York. As a photographer and designer, and with a well-known Indian architect as father, Rahman is uniquely qualified to record India's architectural progression. His sensitivity to the creativity of non-Western cultures has earned him prestigious commissions, including the photography of submissions for the Agha Khan Award. His photos are on pages 8, 20 and 21, 92 and 93, 96, 208, 212–213, 216, 218, 220–221, 222 and 223, 224–225, 226 and 227.

God is love.

Is this the final message of India?

E.M. Forster